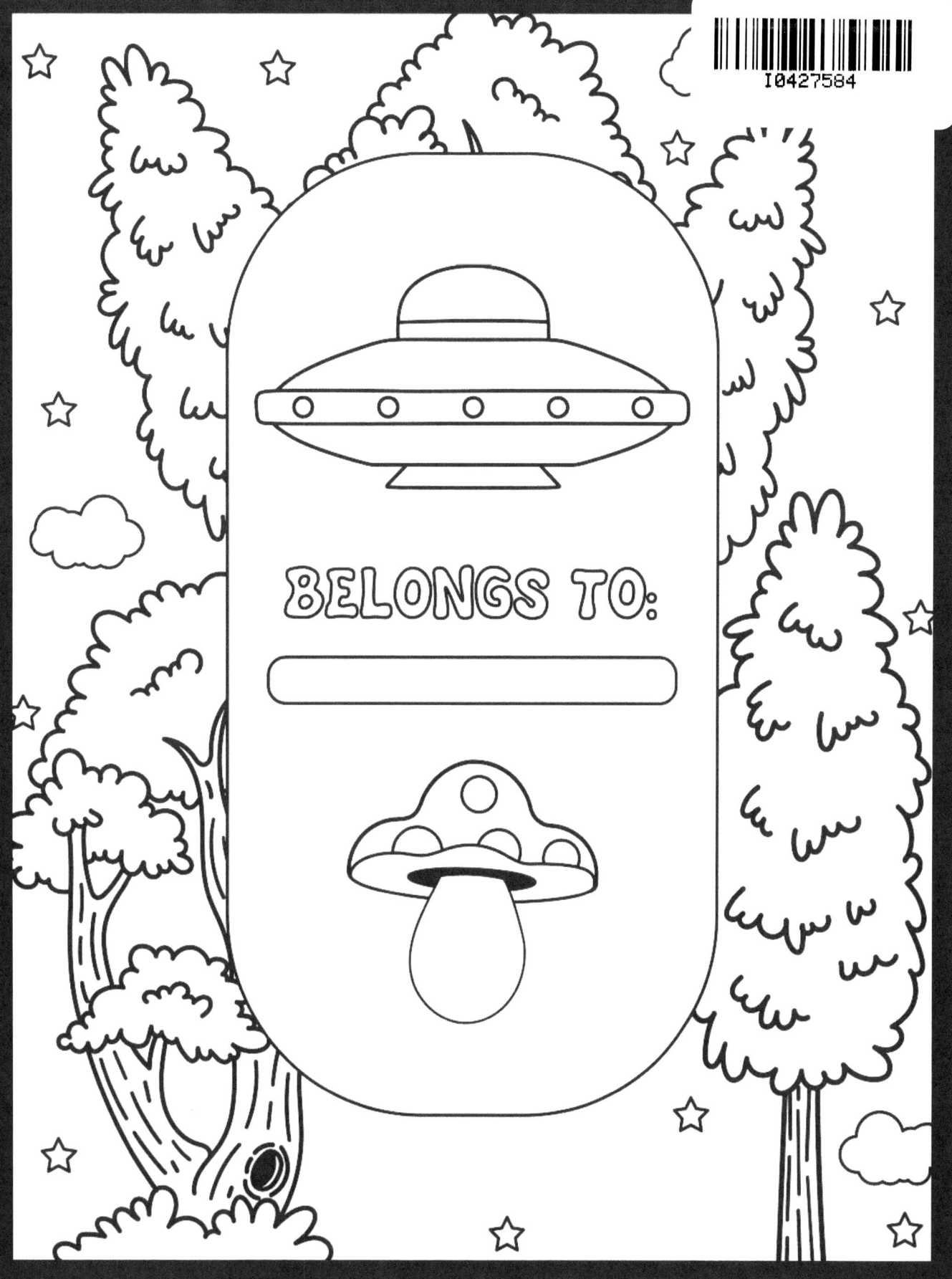

BELONGS TO:

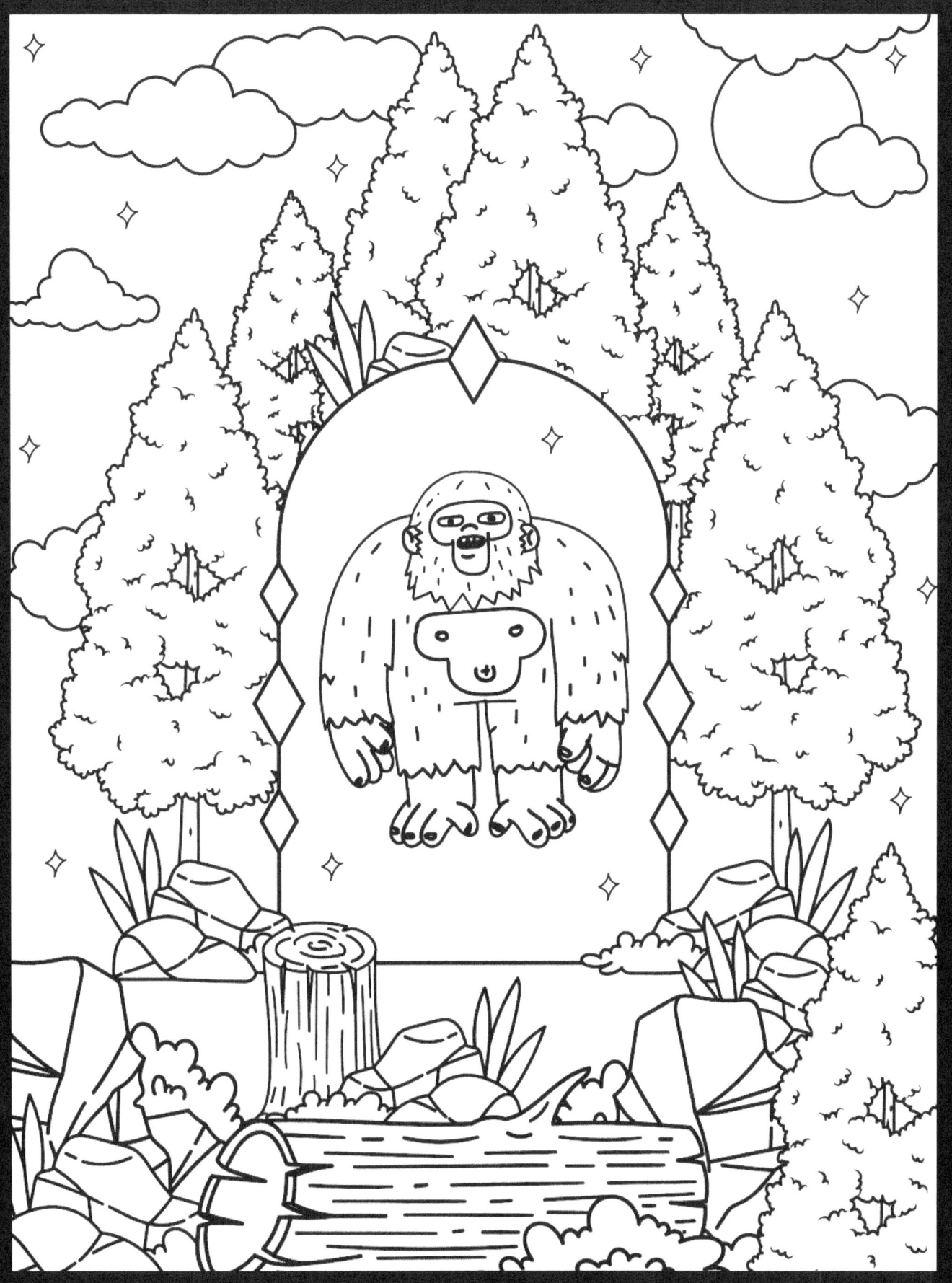

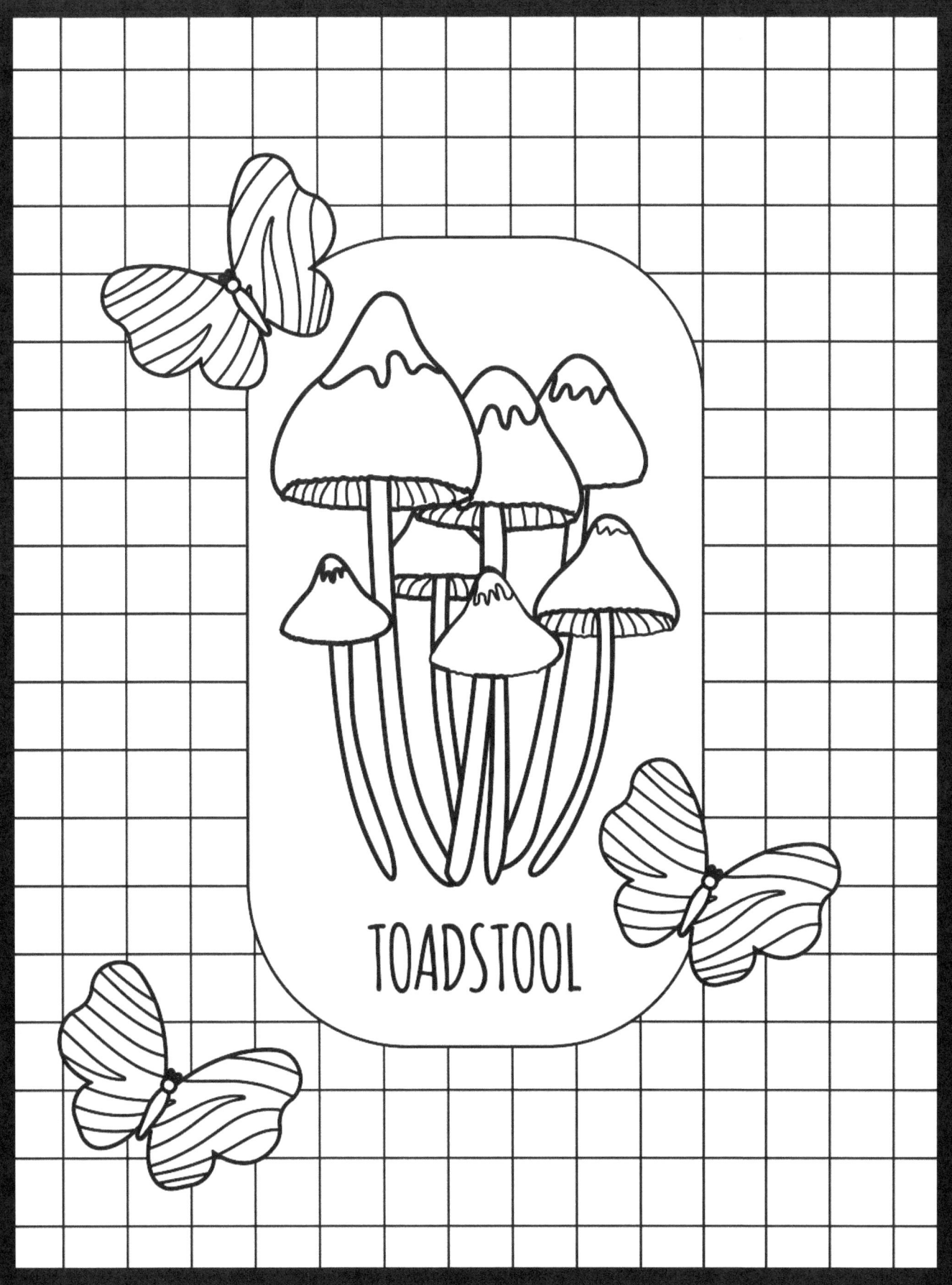

TOADSTOOL

TOADSTOOL

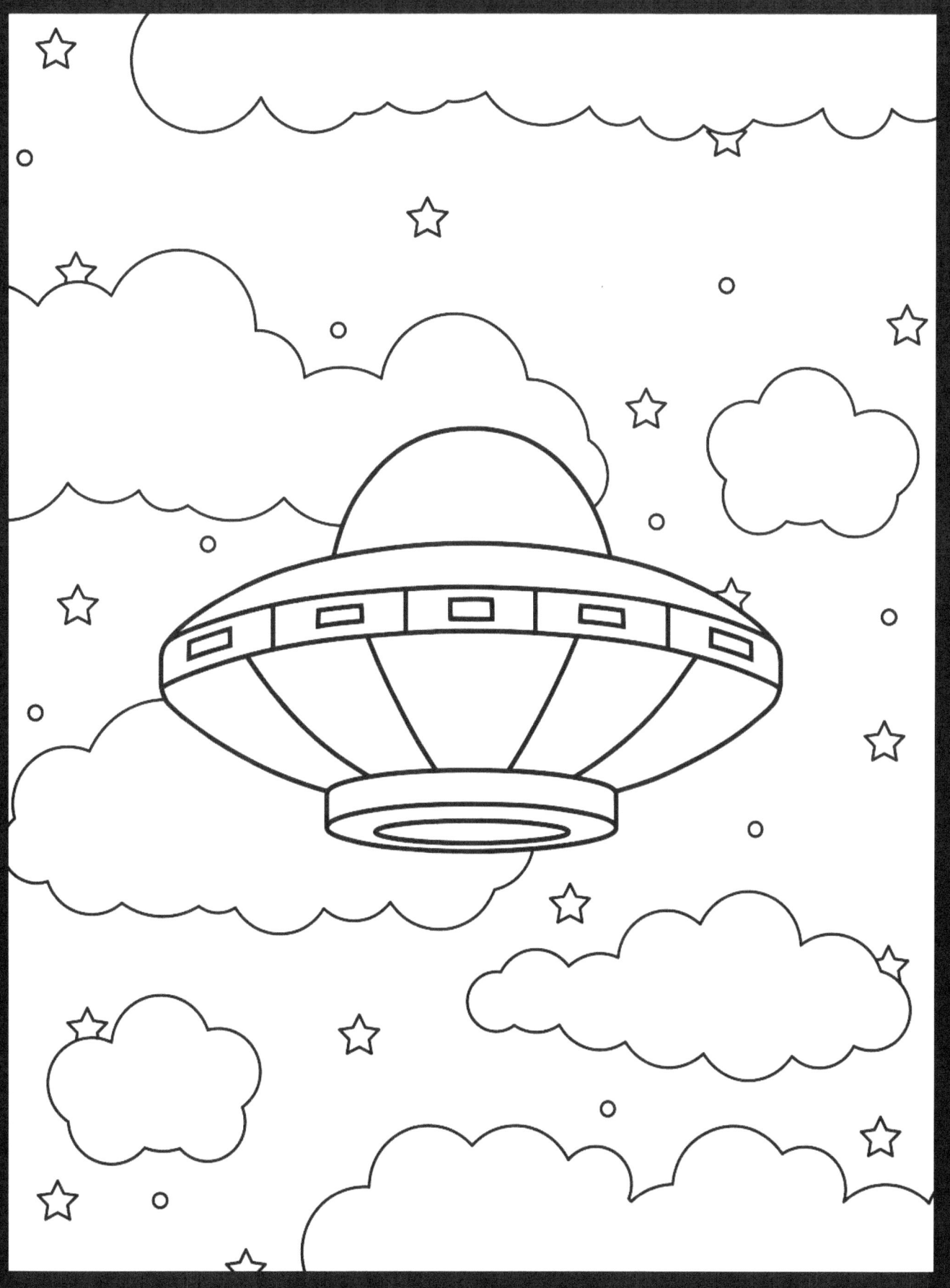

THEY ARE HERE

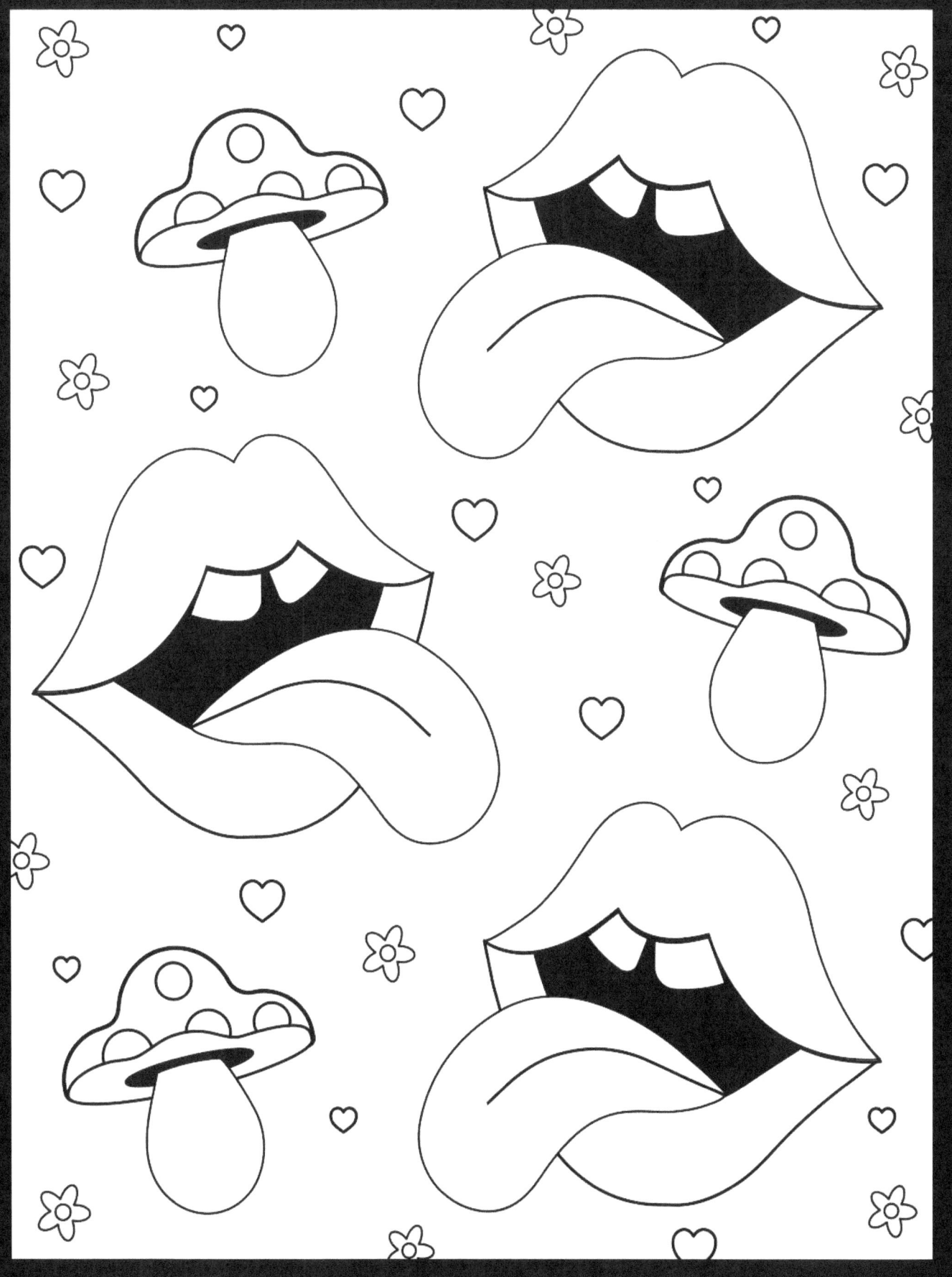

OPEN WIDE

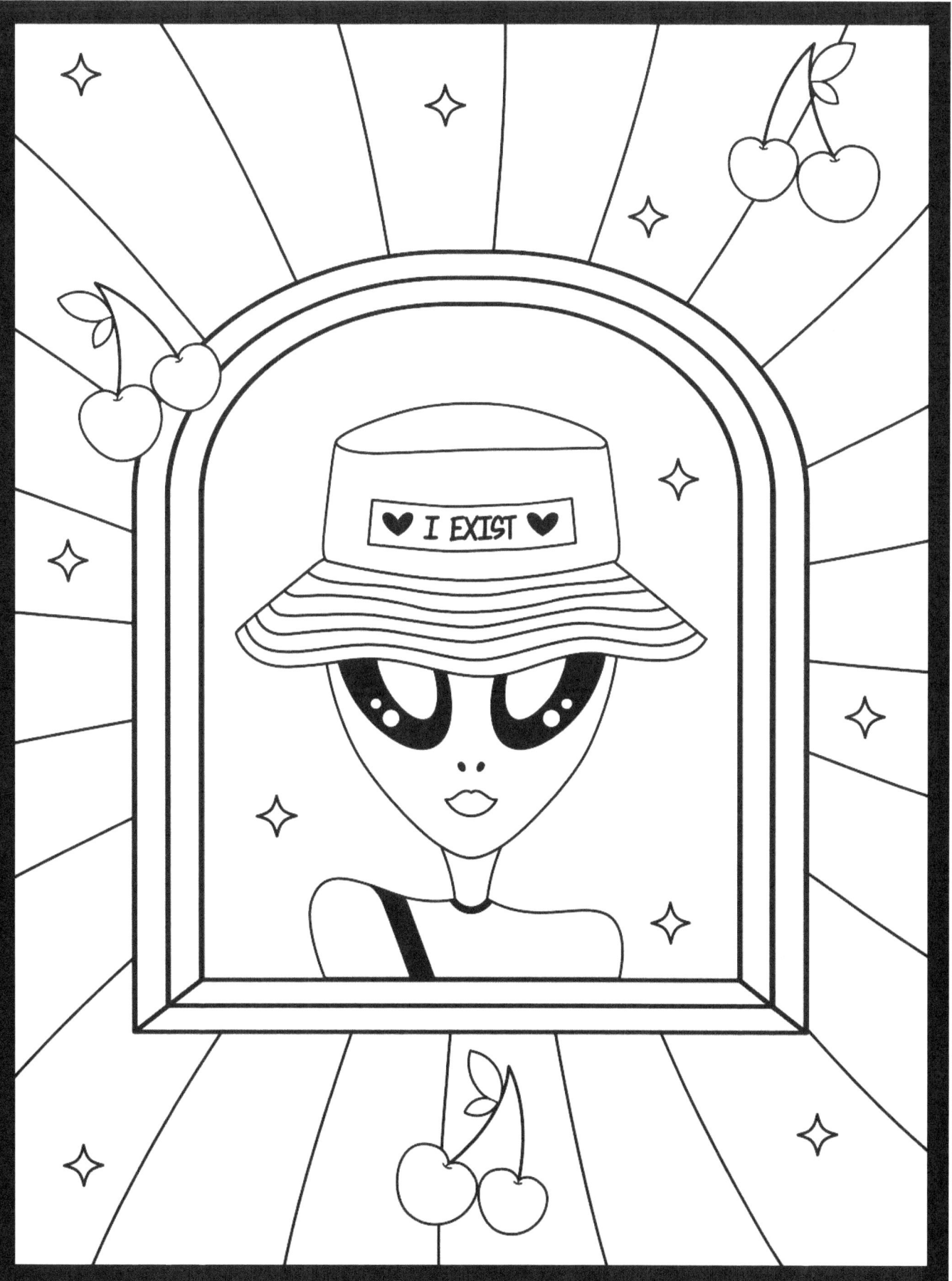

I EXIST

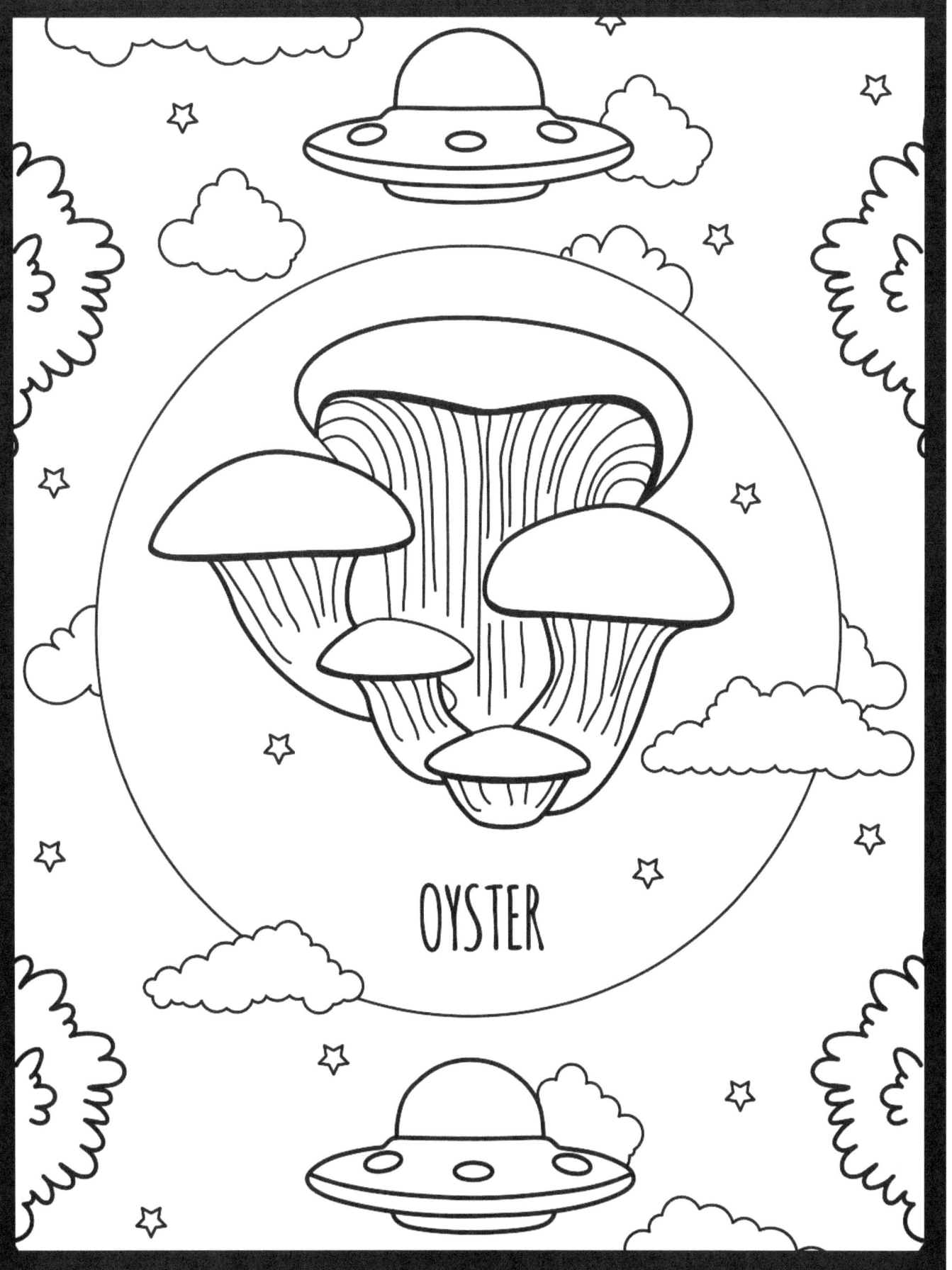

OYSTER

OYSTER

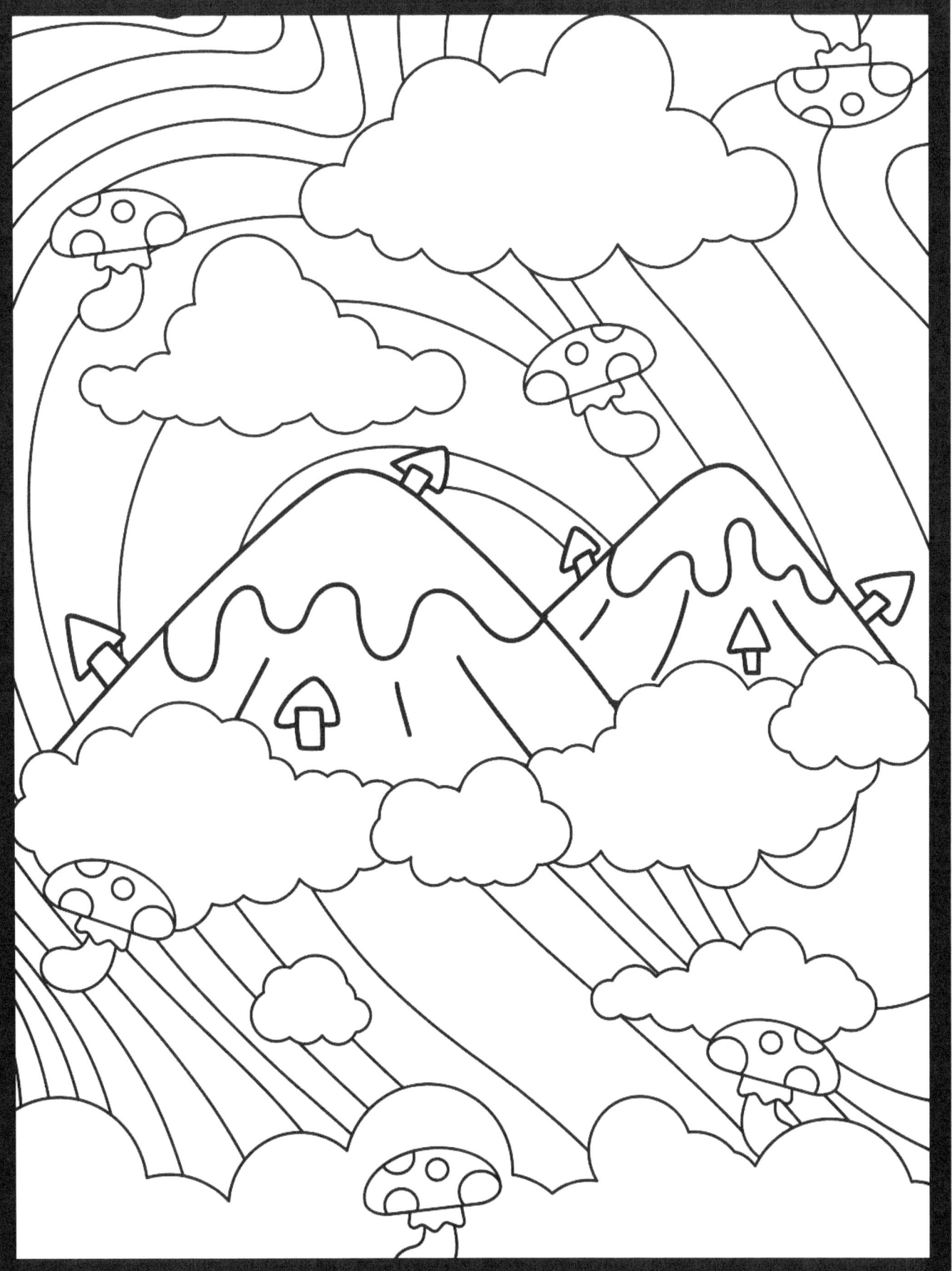

MAGIC MOUNTAINS

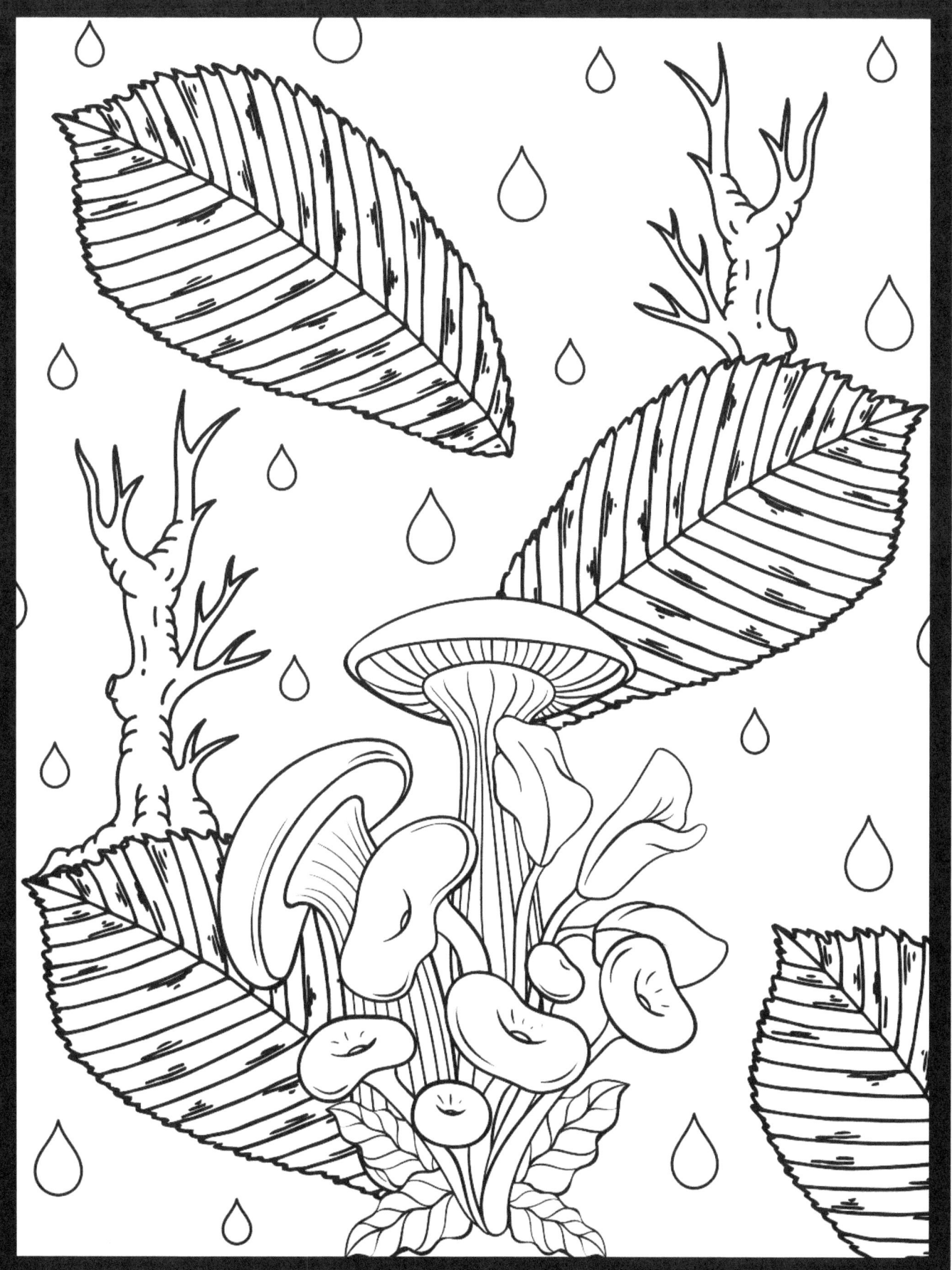

CYCLES

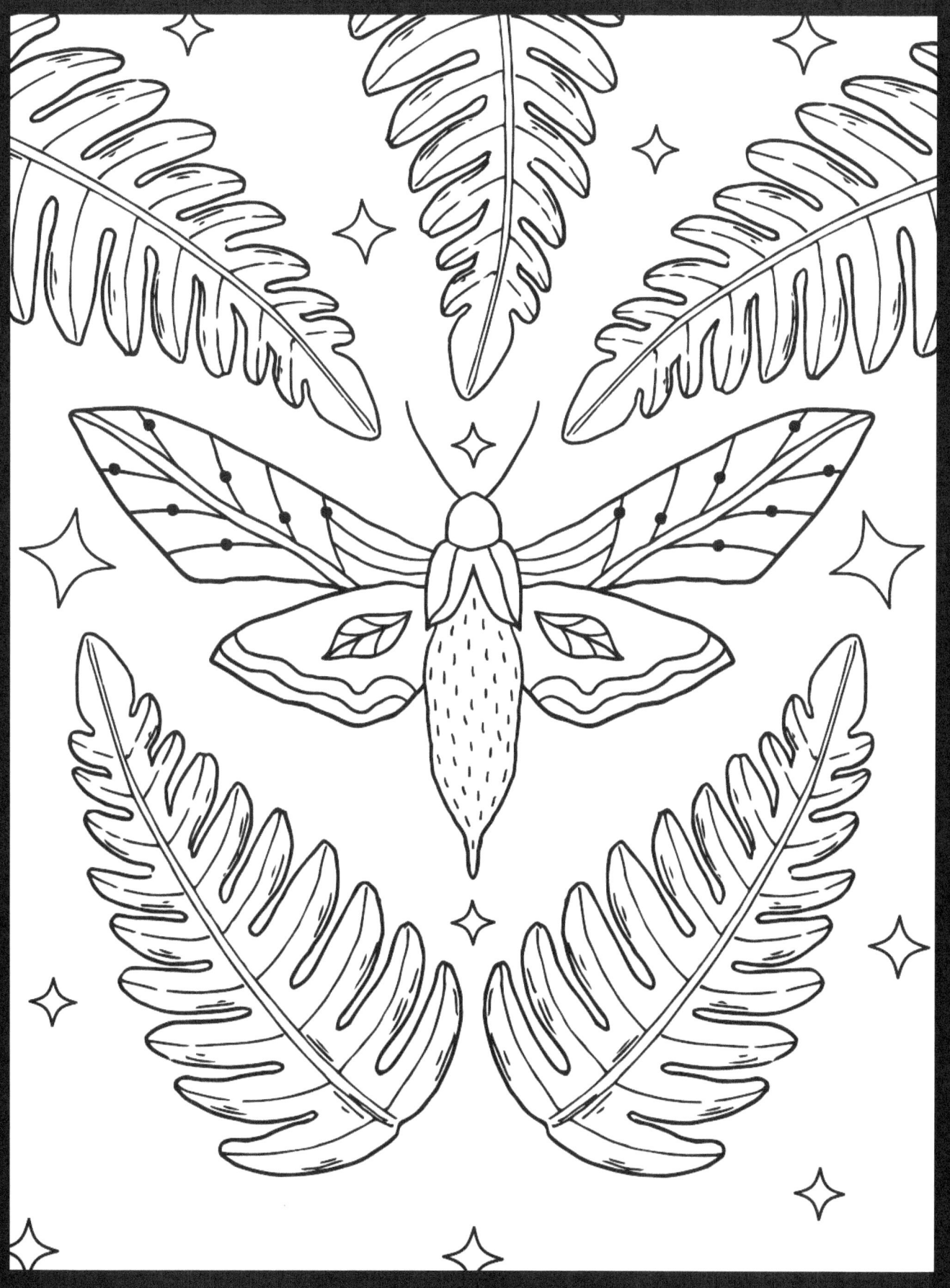

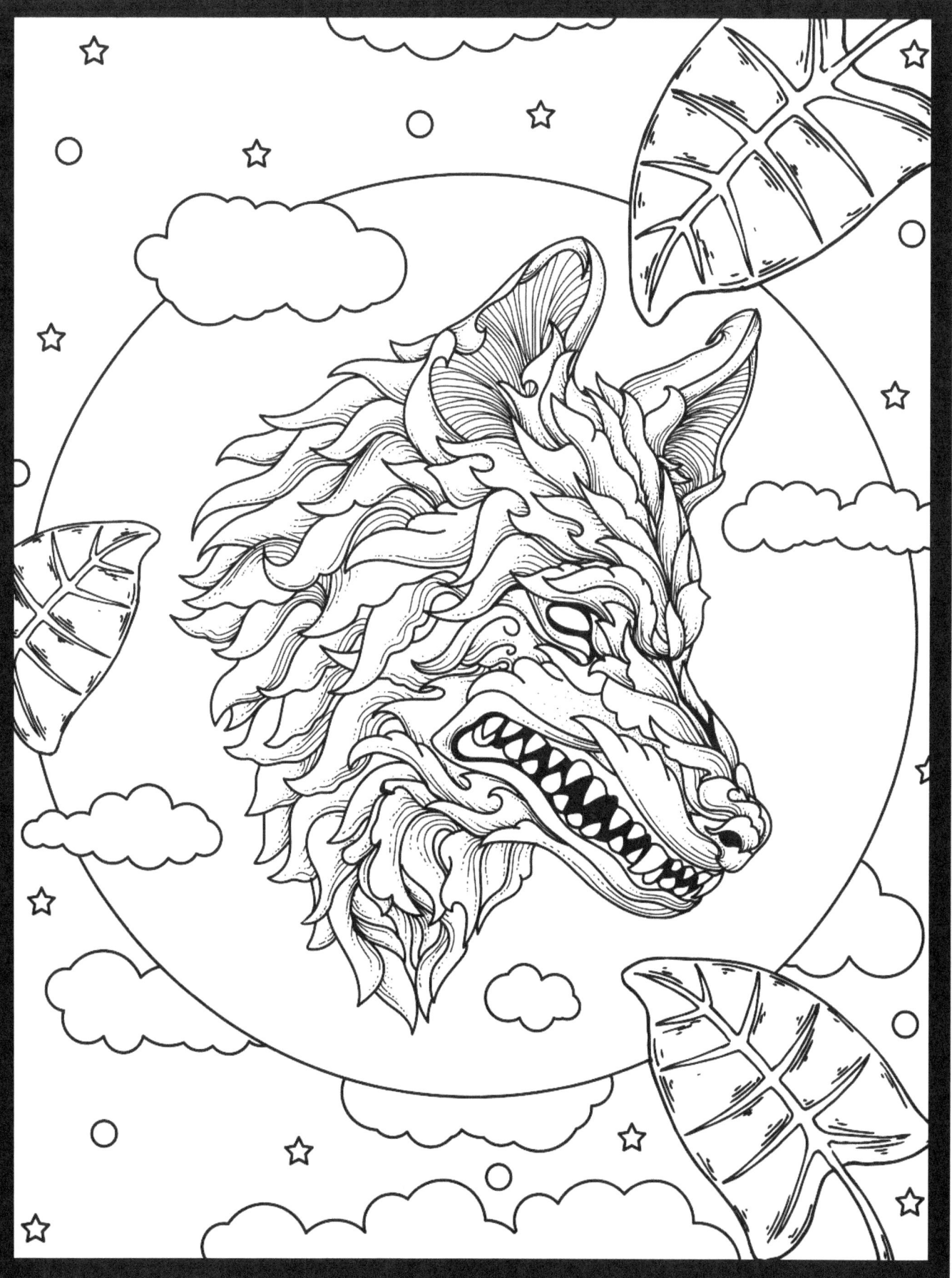

DOGMAN

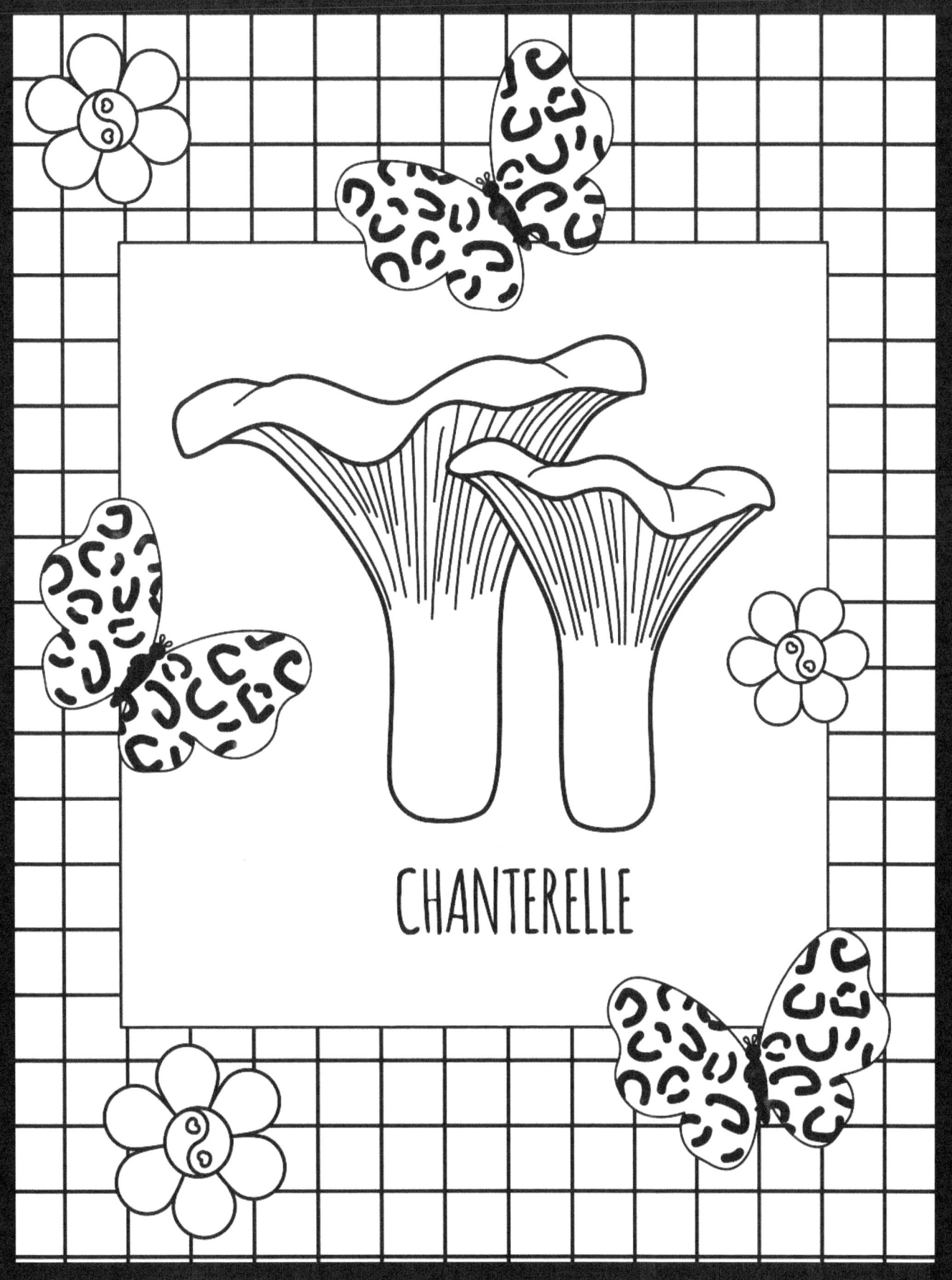

CHANTERELLE

CHANTERELLE

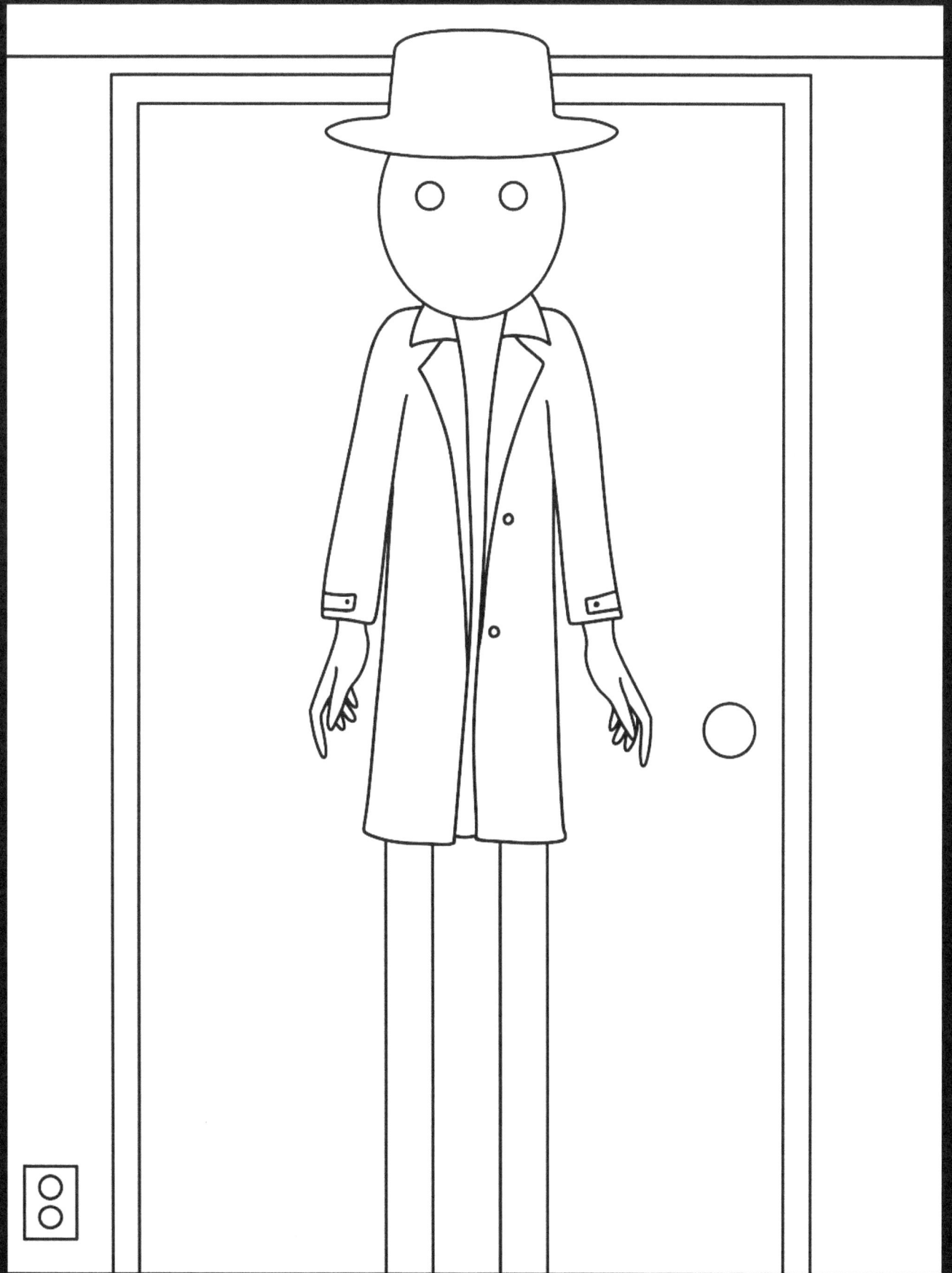

HAVE YOU SEEN HATMAN?

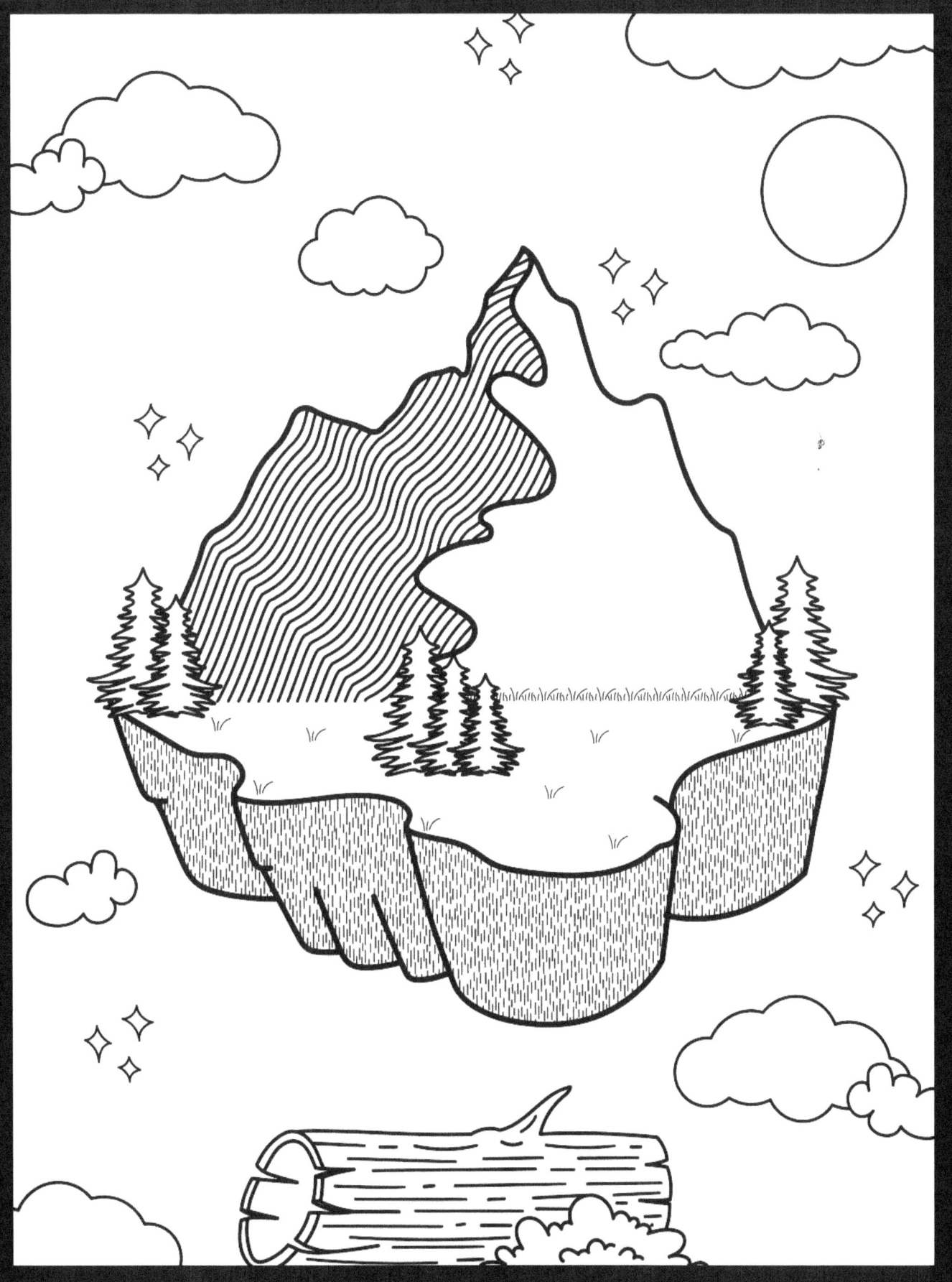

SKY SCENES

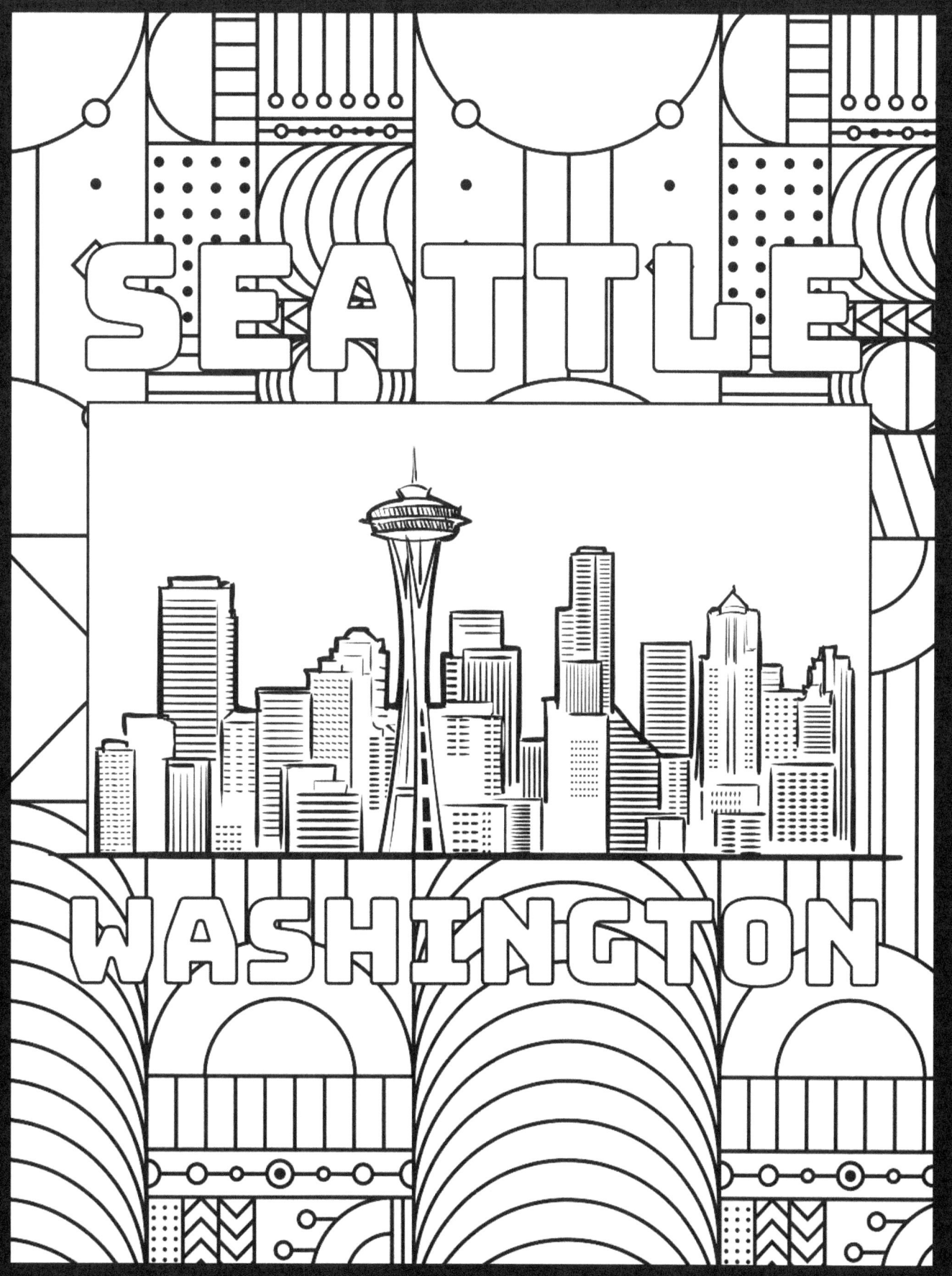

SEATTLE

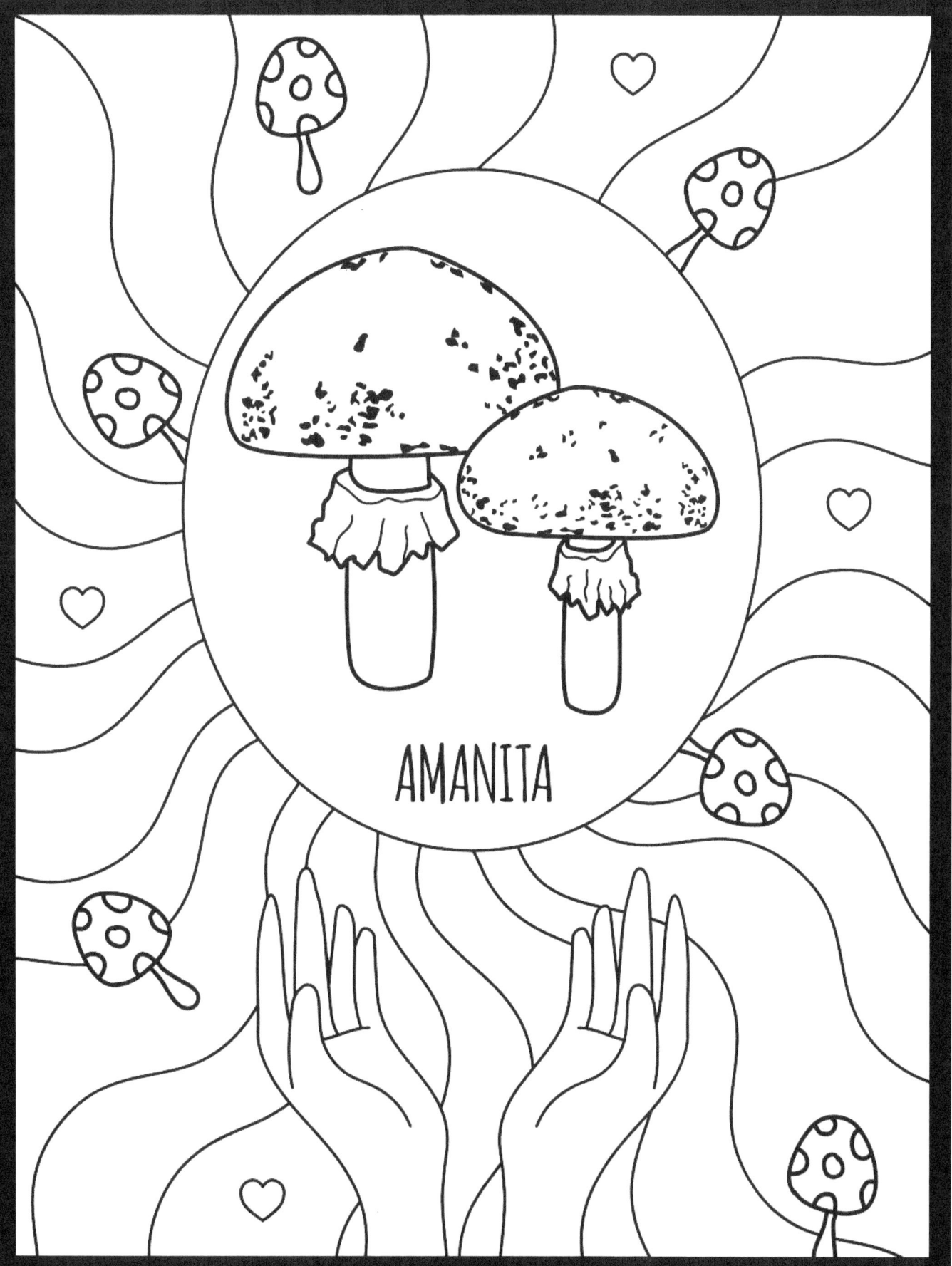

AMANITA

AMANITA

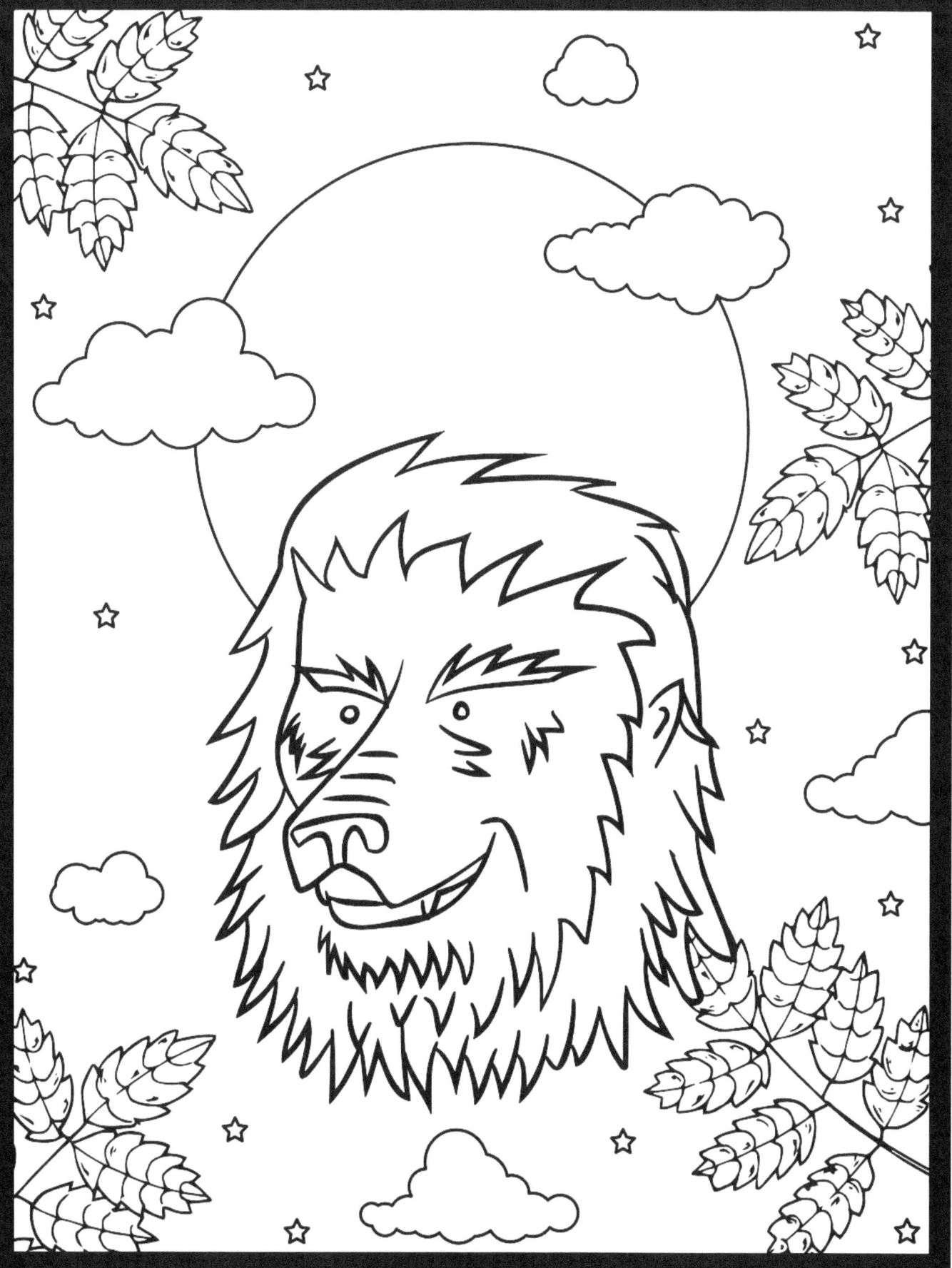

WEREWOLF

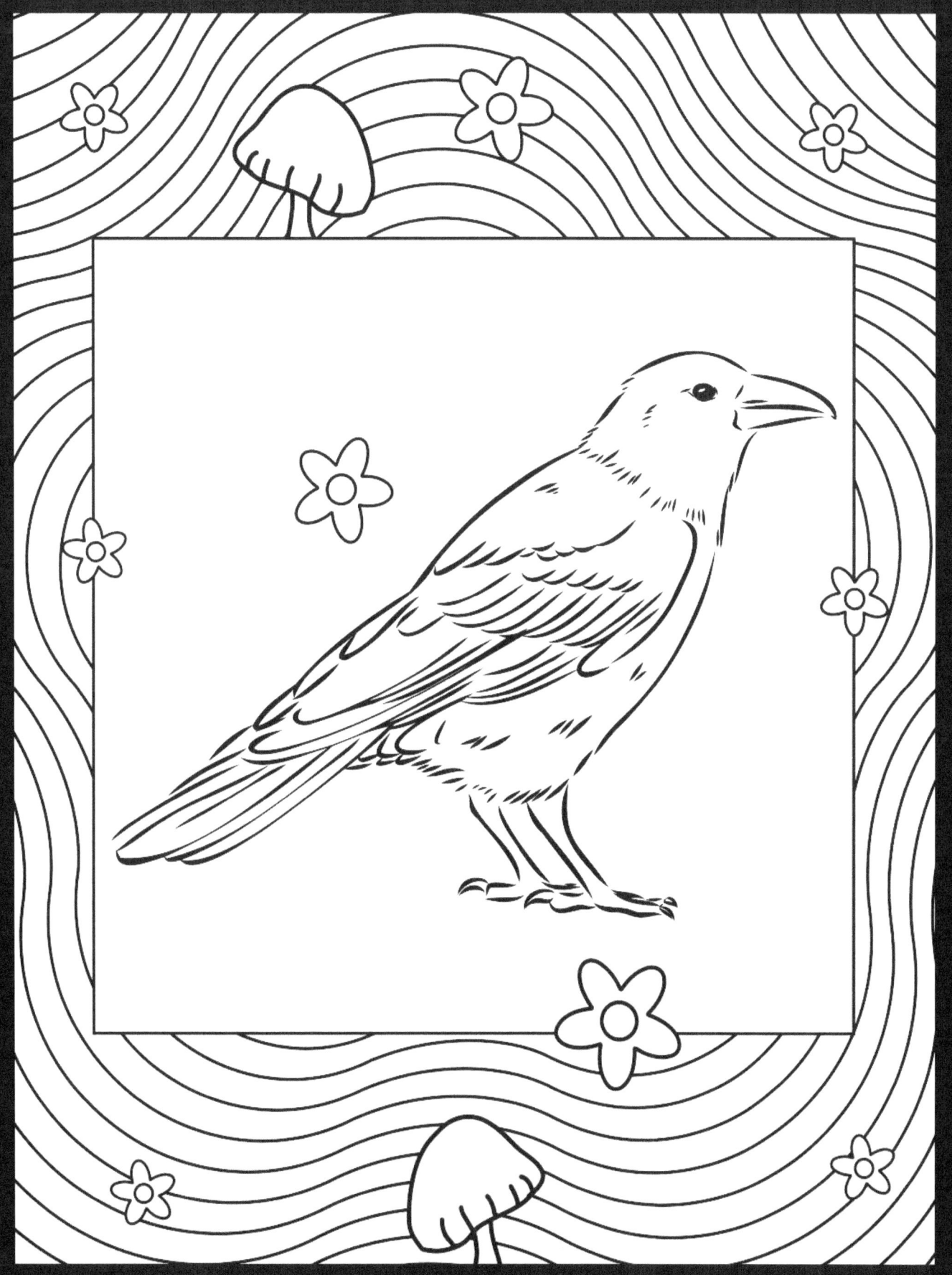

CROW BRO

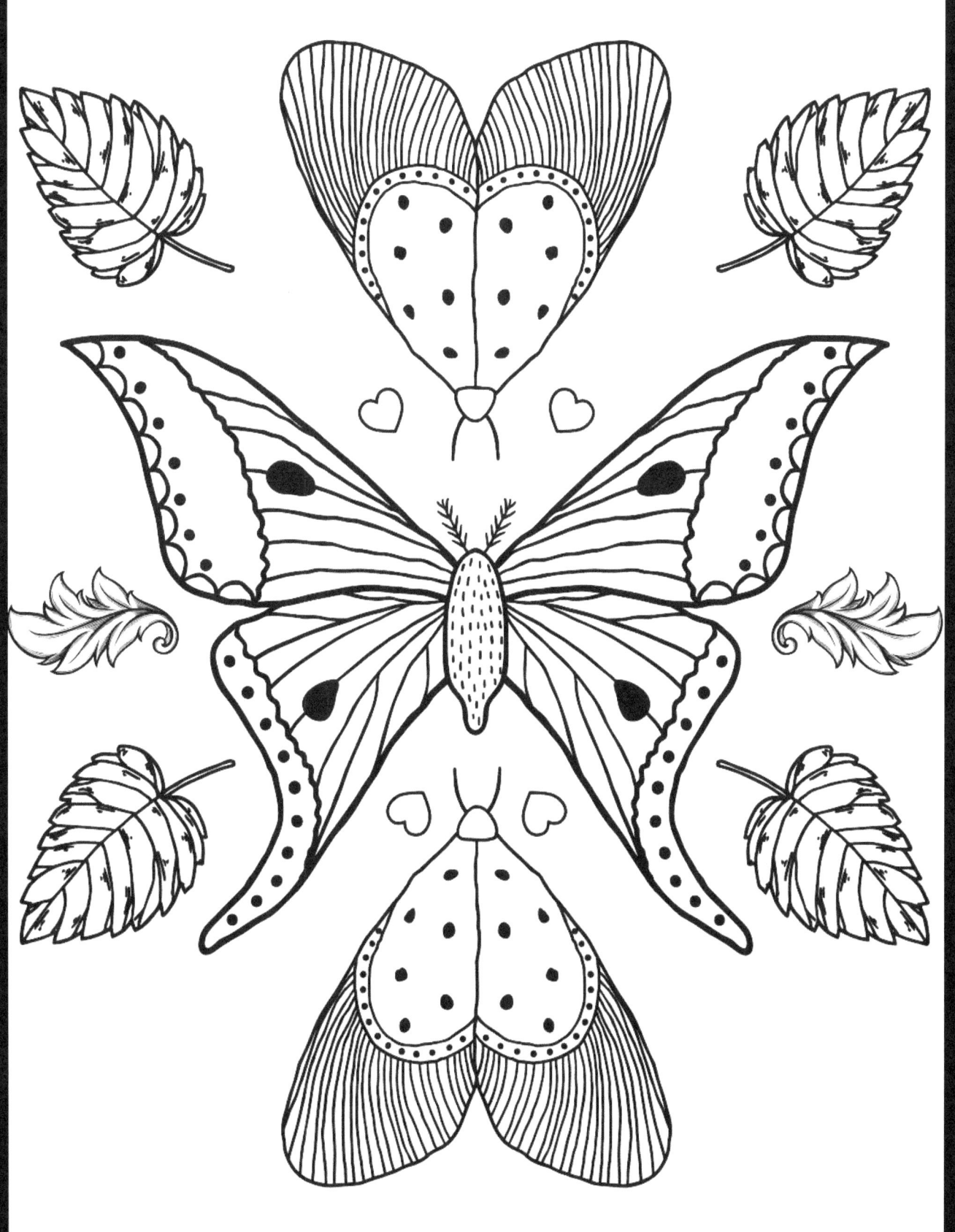

THINGS THAT FLY

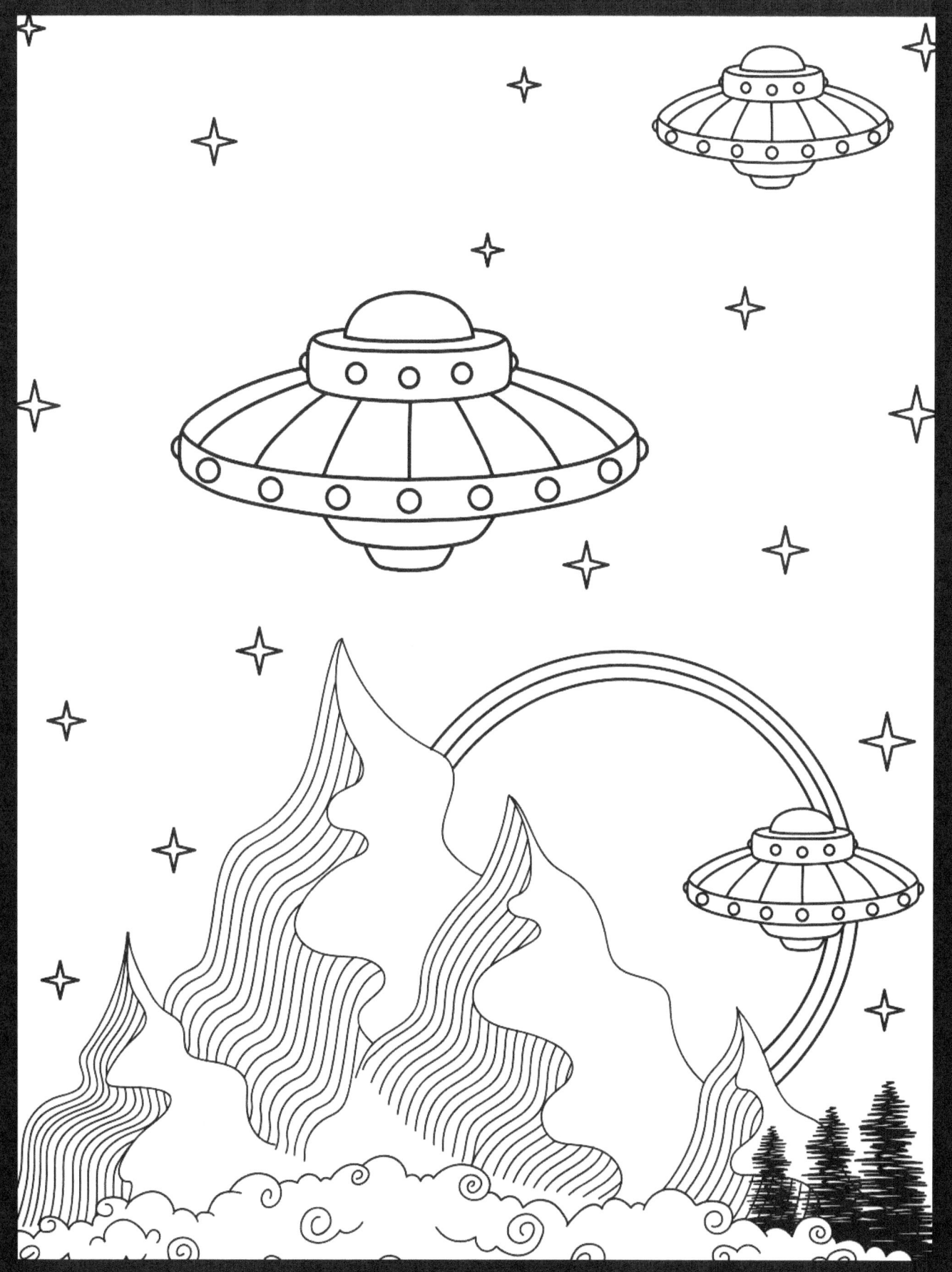

FORMATION

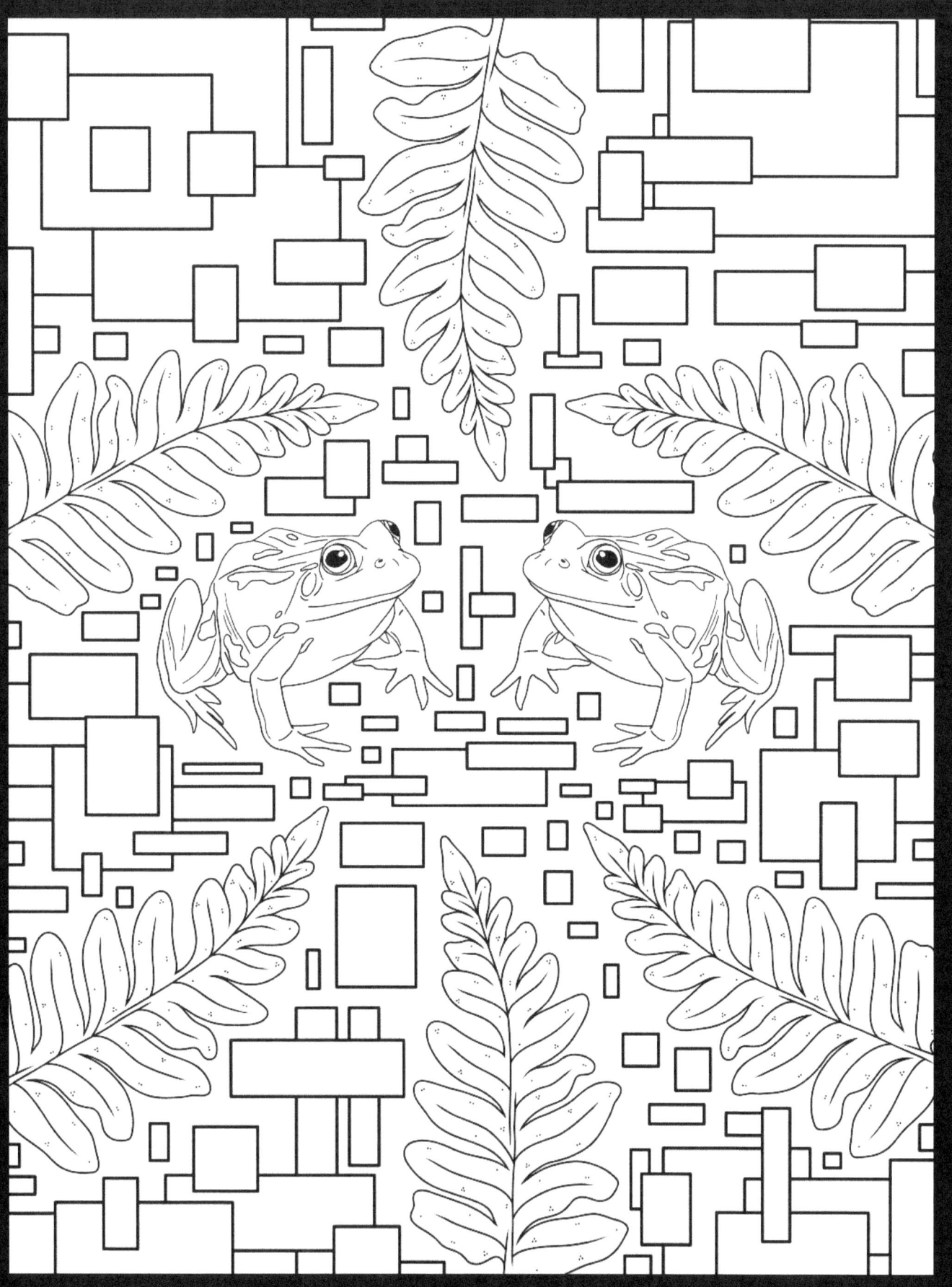

FROGS

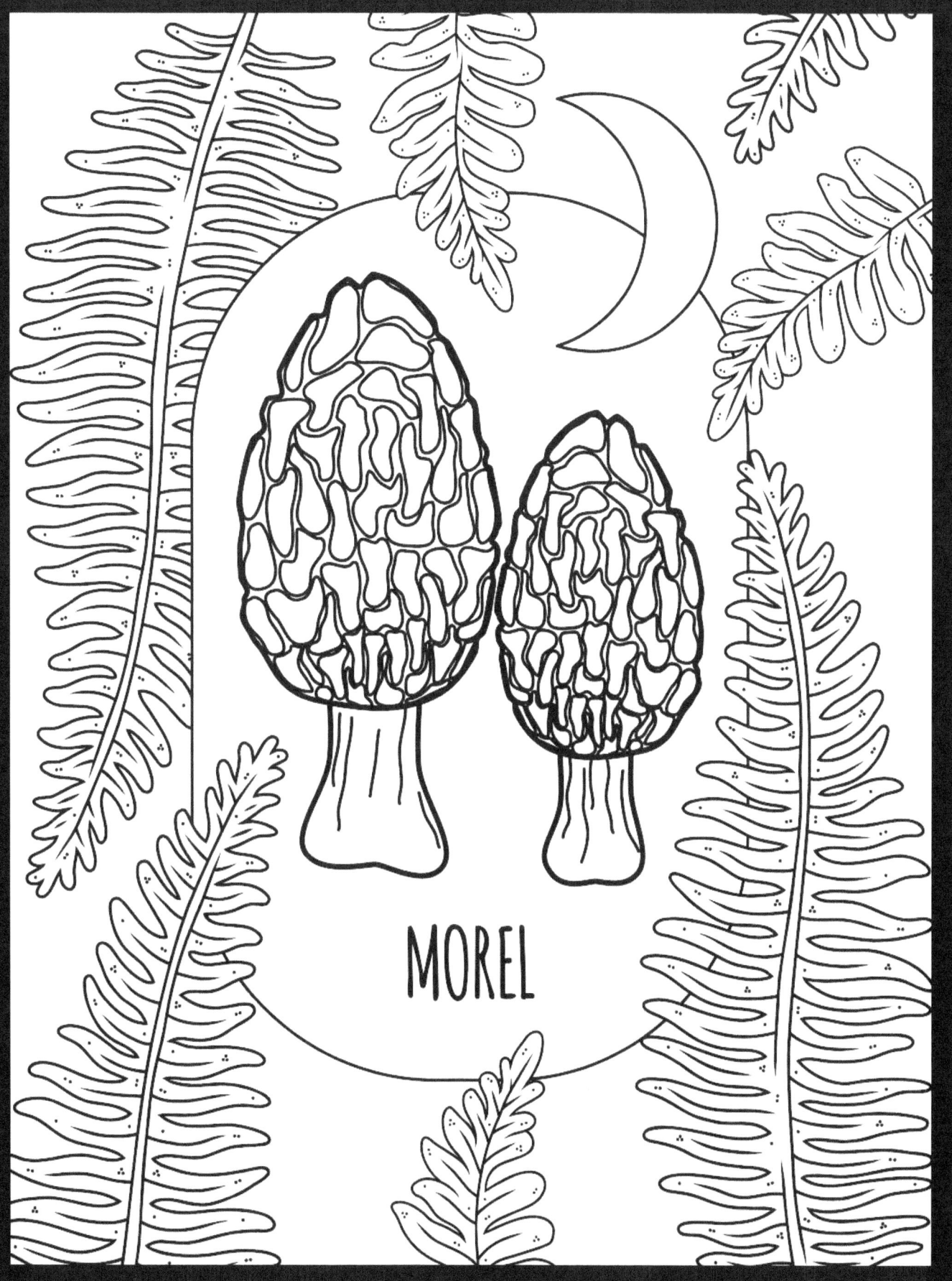

MOREL

MOREL

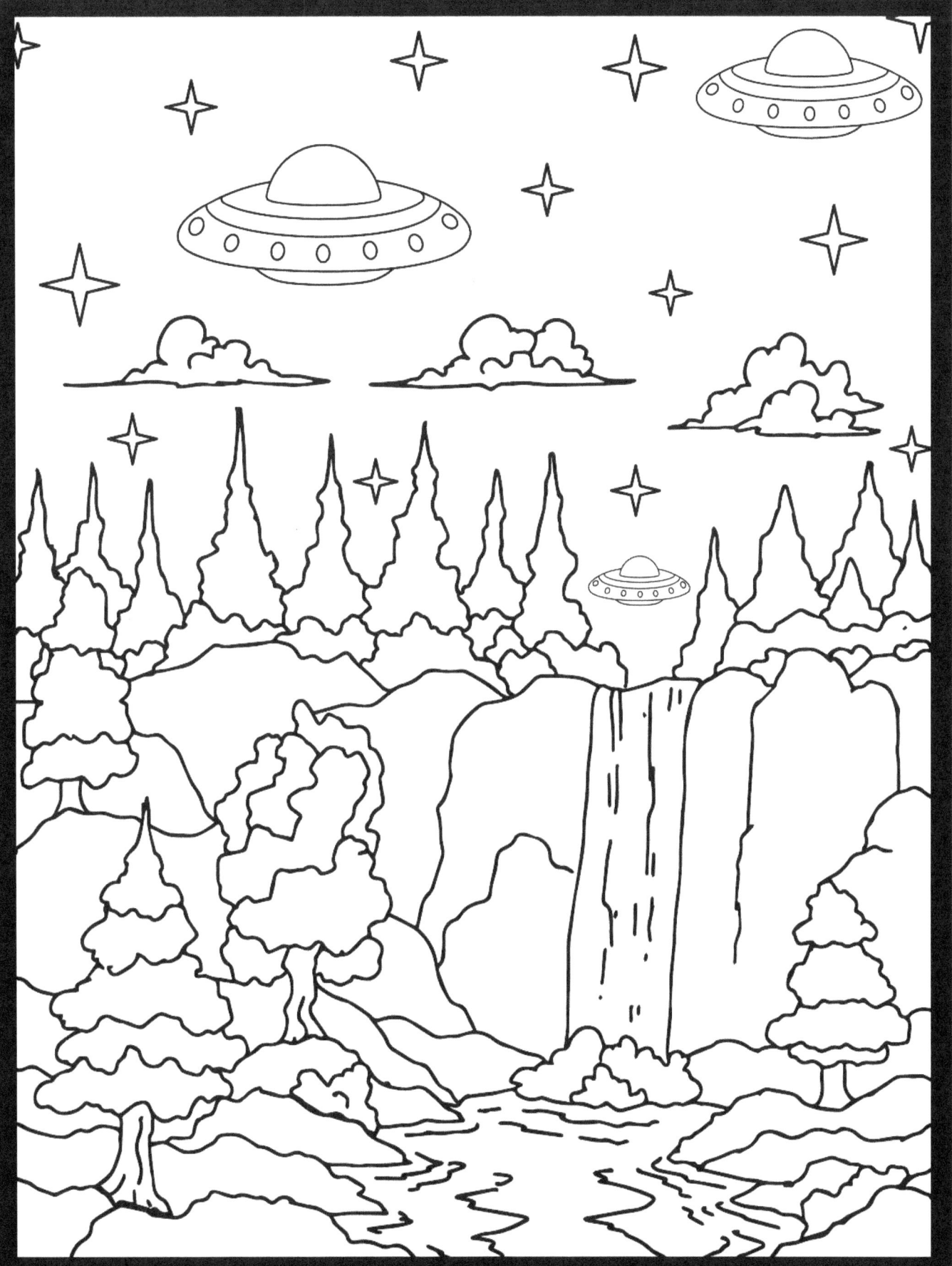

CHASING WATERFALLS

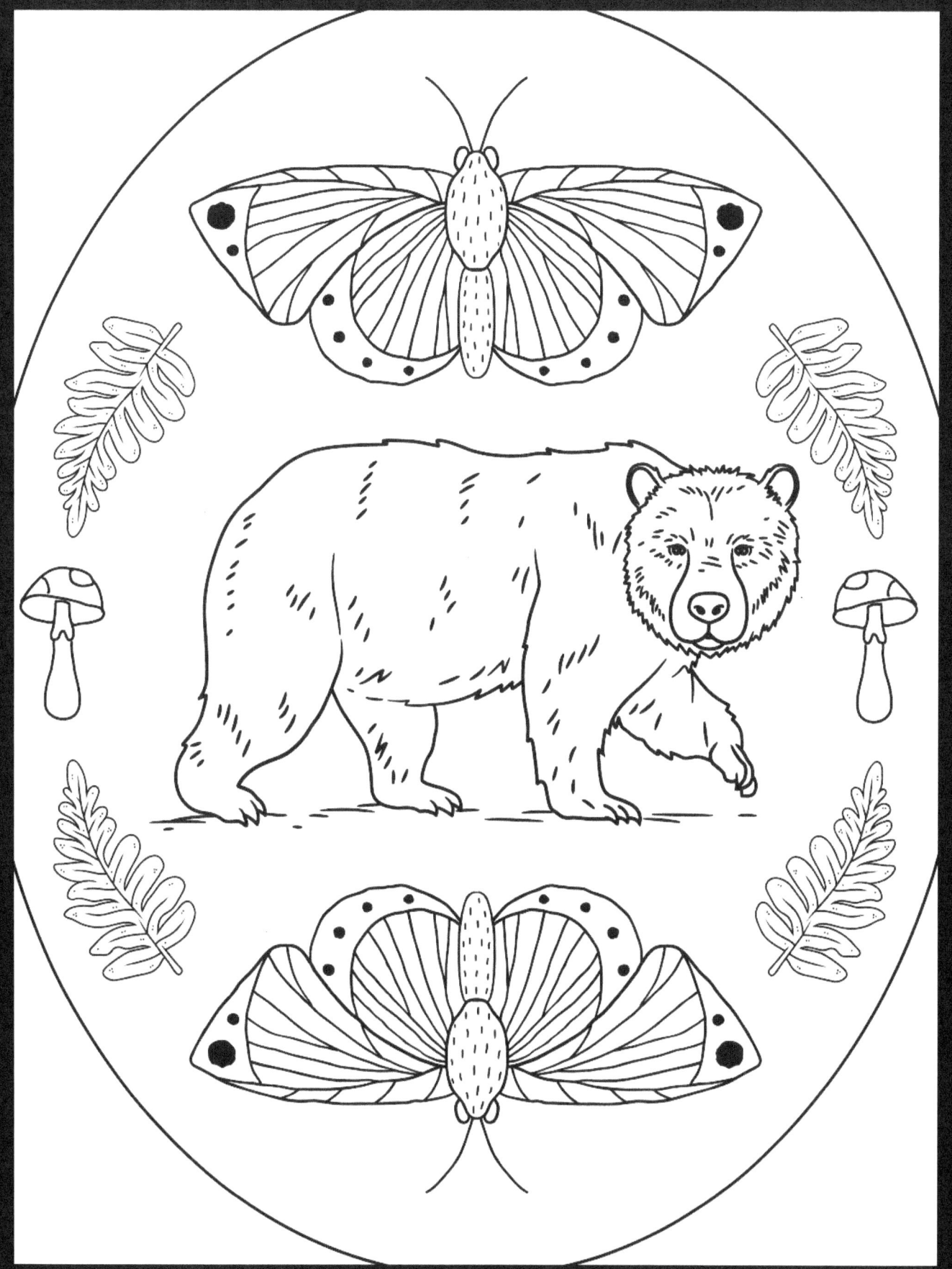

BEAR

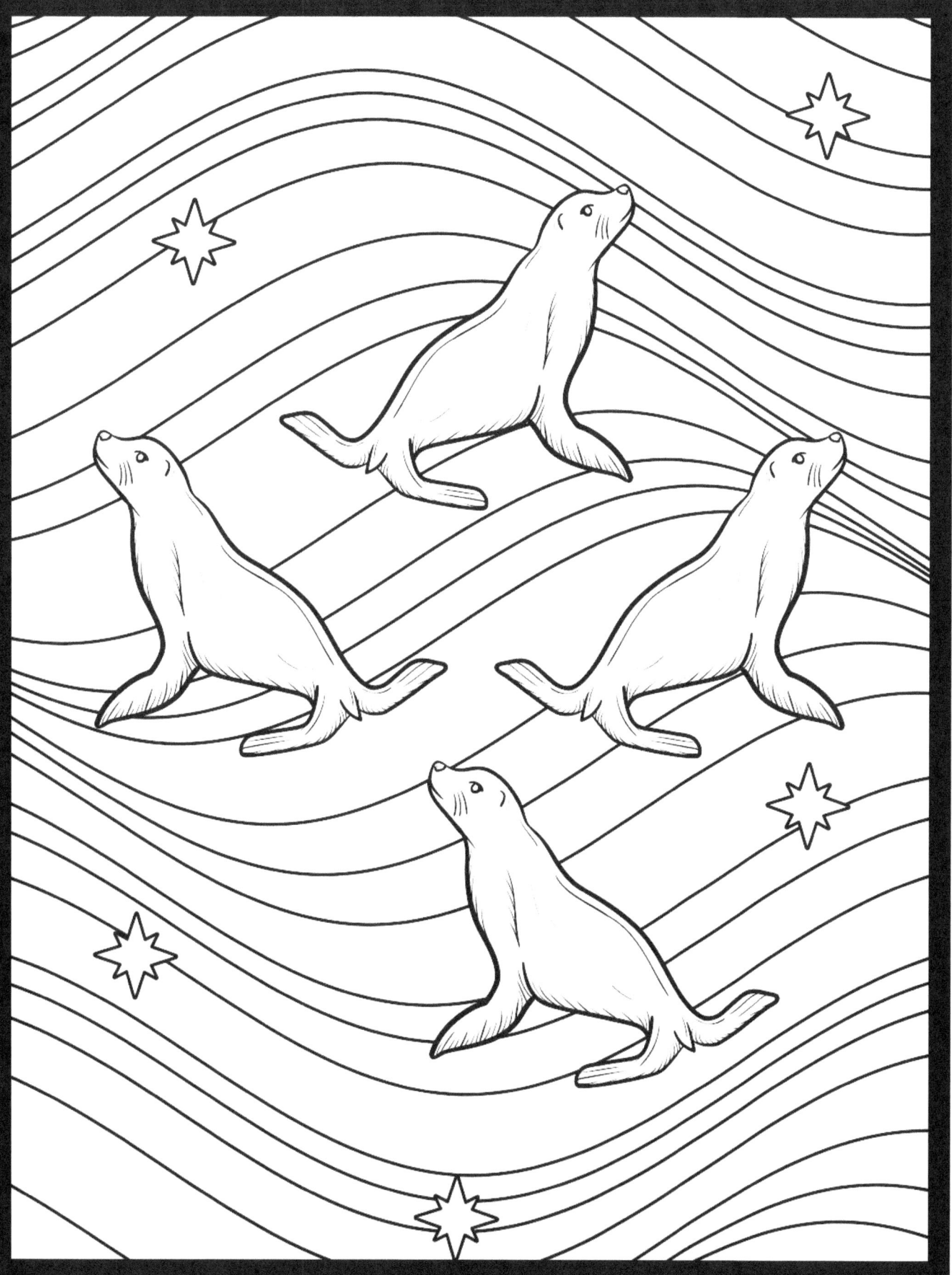

SEALS

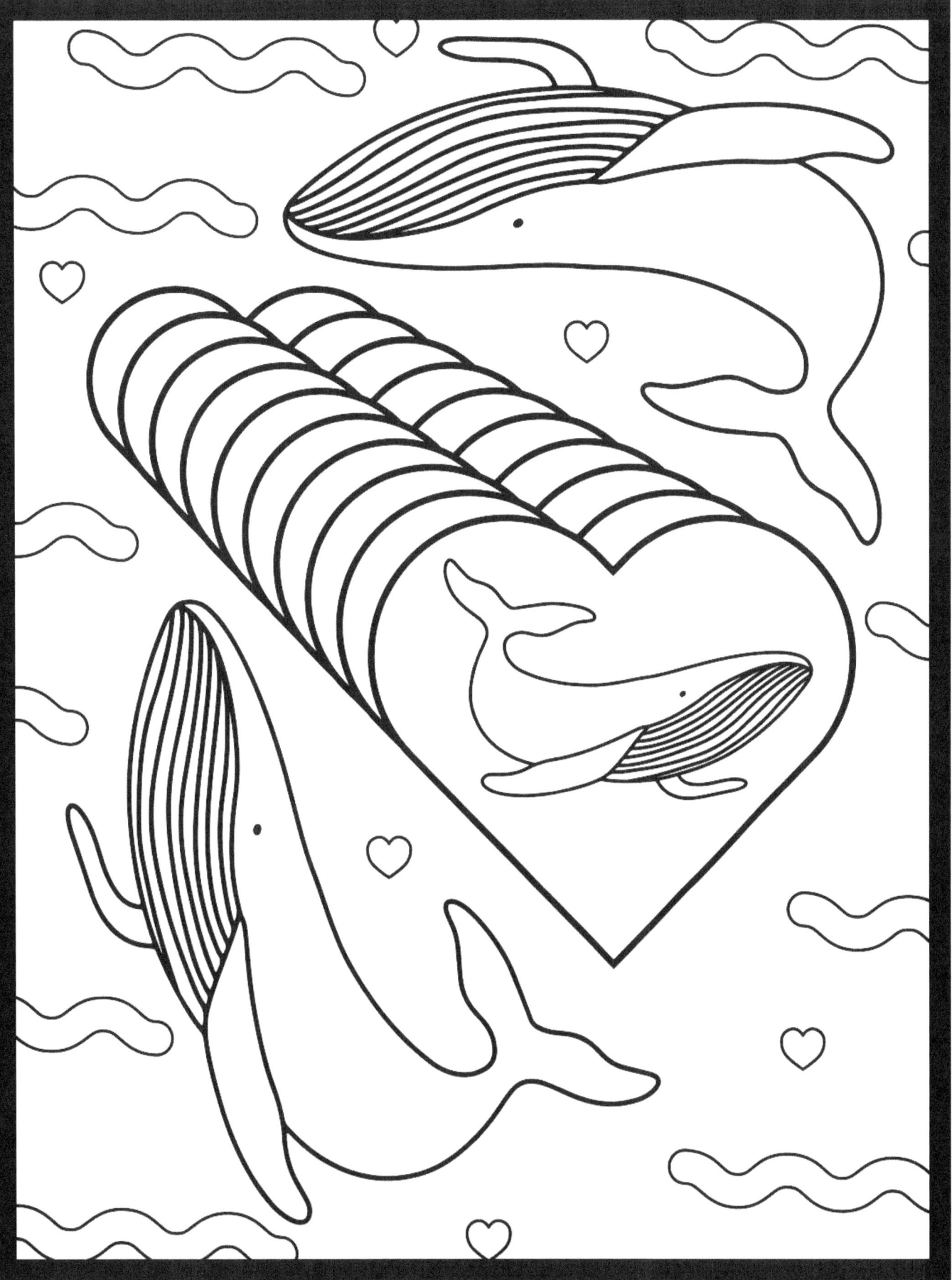

WHALES

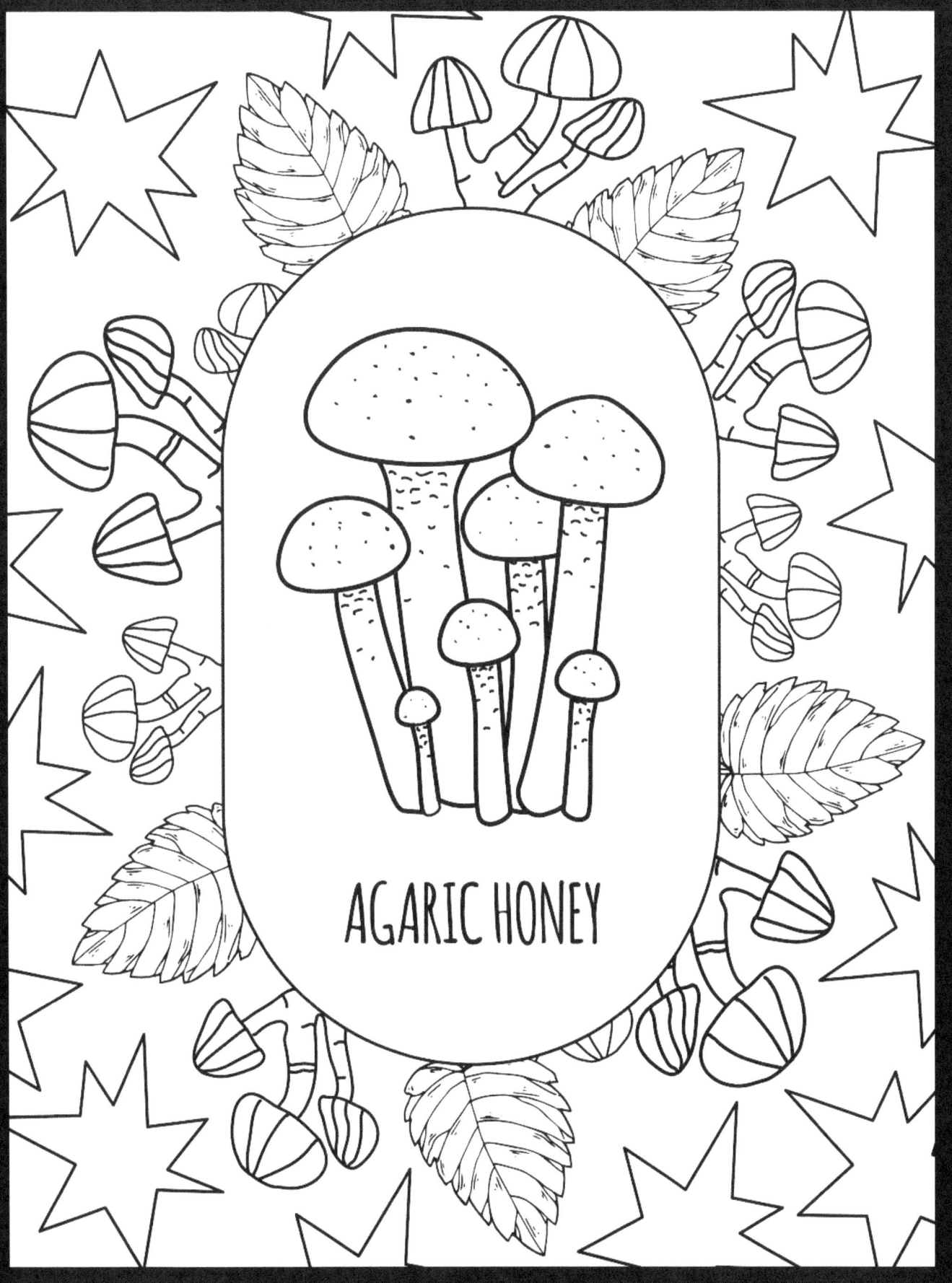

AGARIC HONEY

AGARIC HONEY

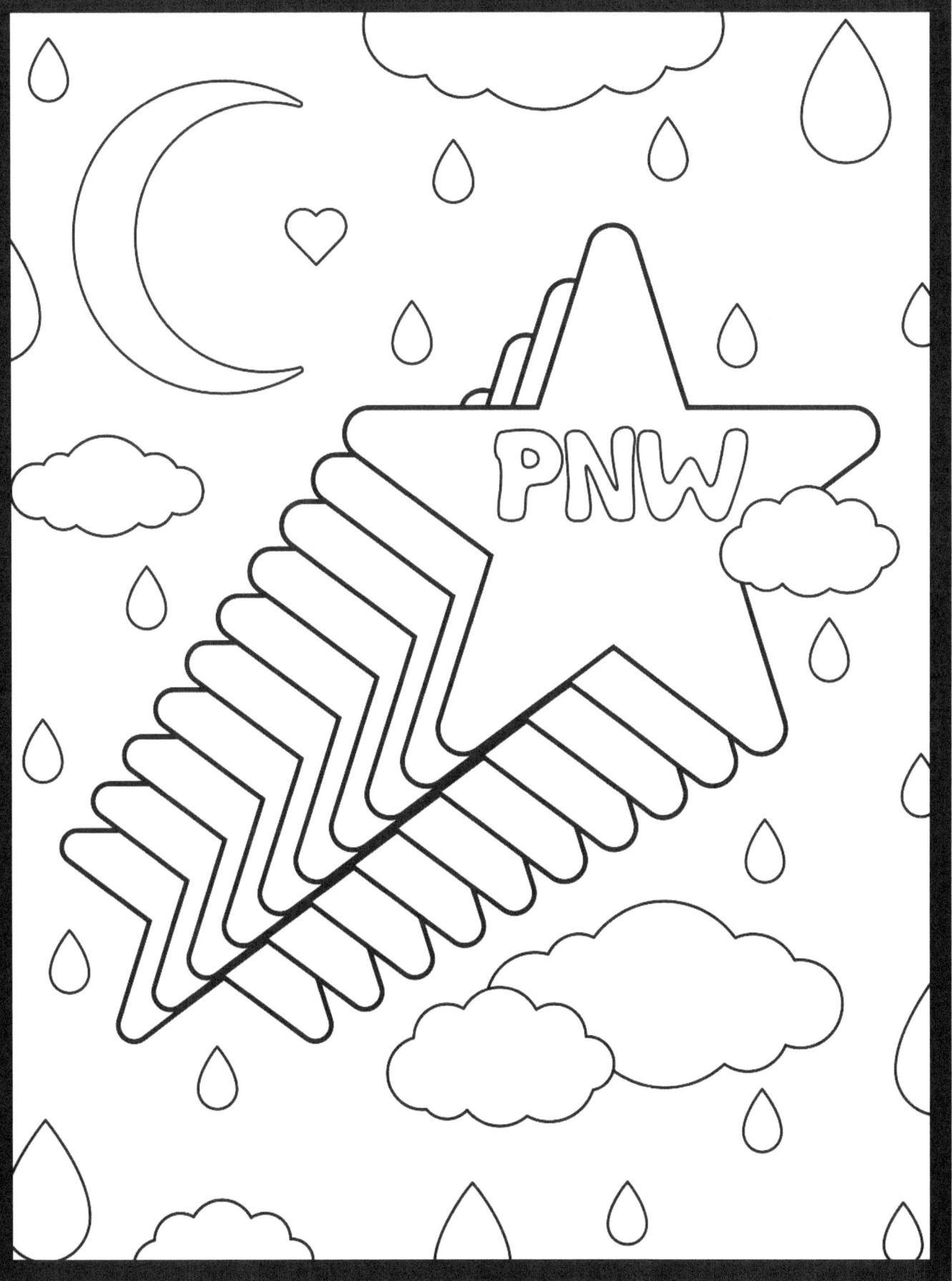

PNW

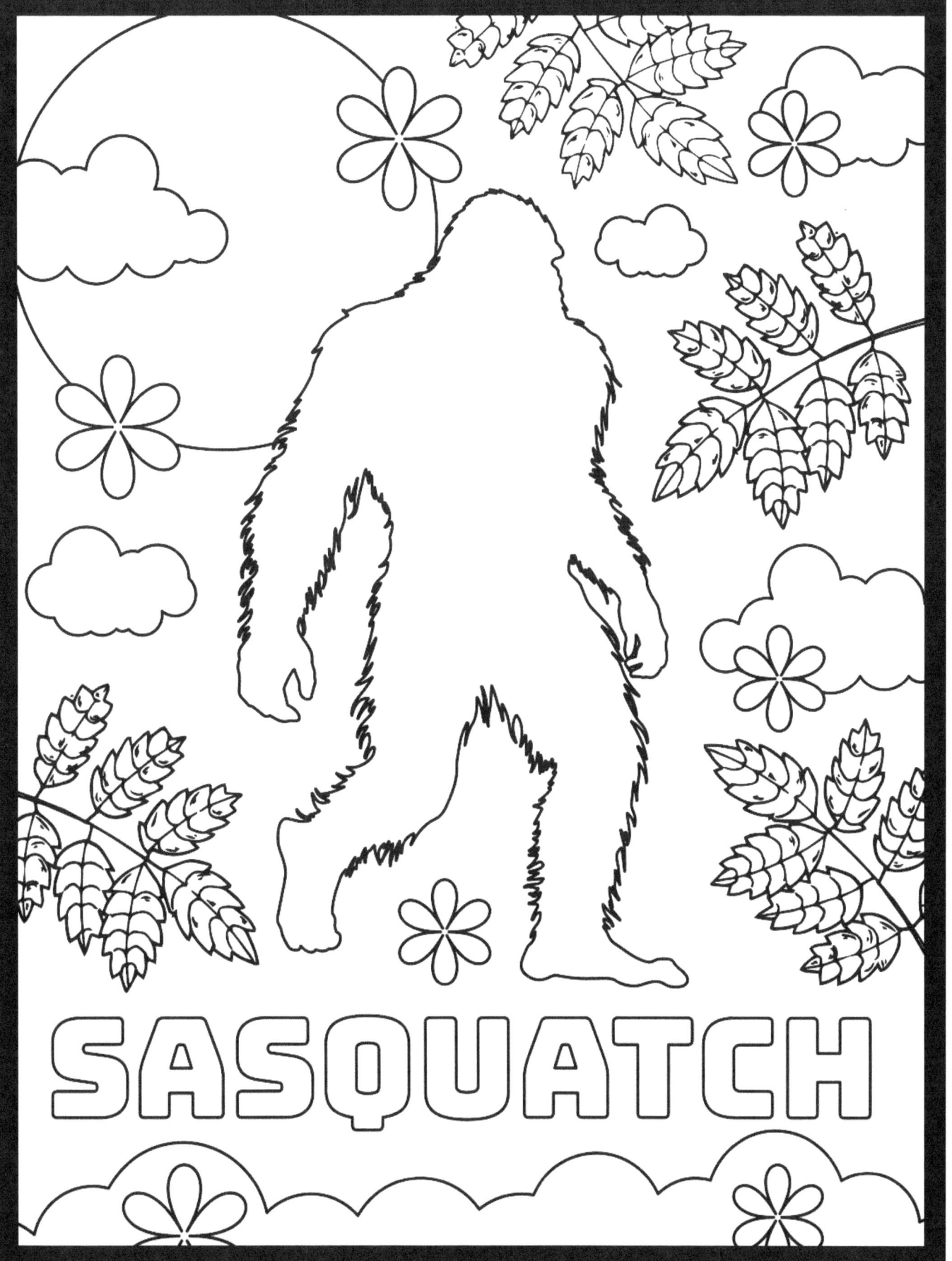

SASQUATCH

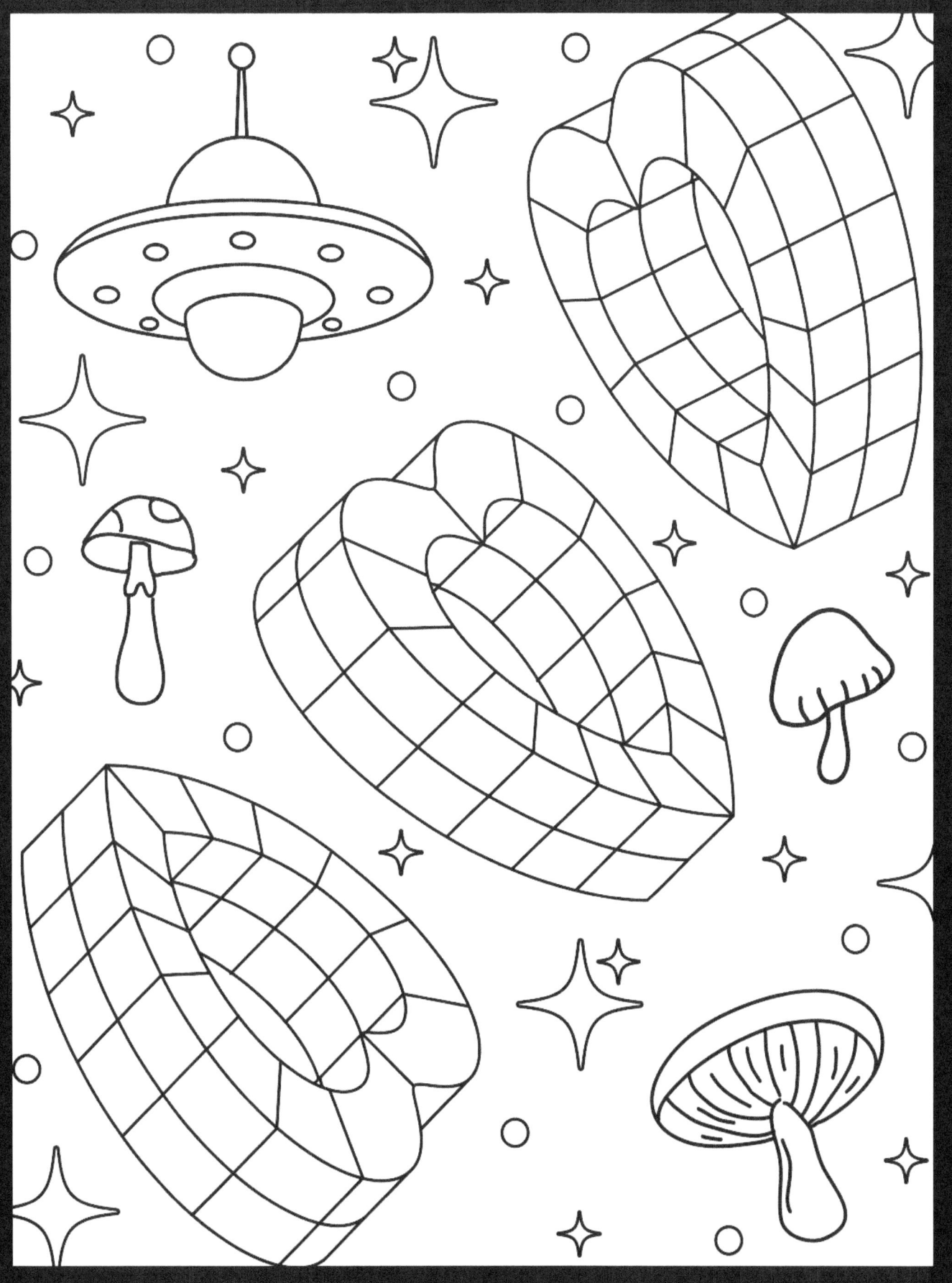

TRANSPORTATION METHODS

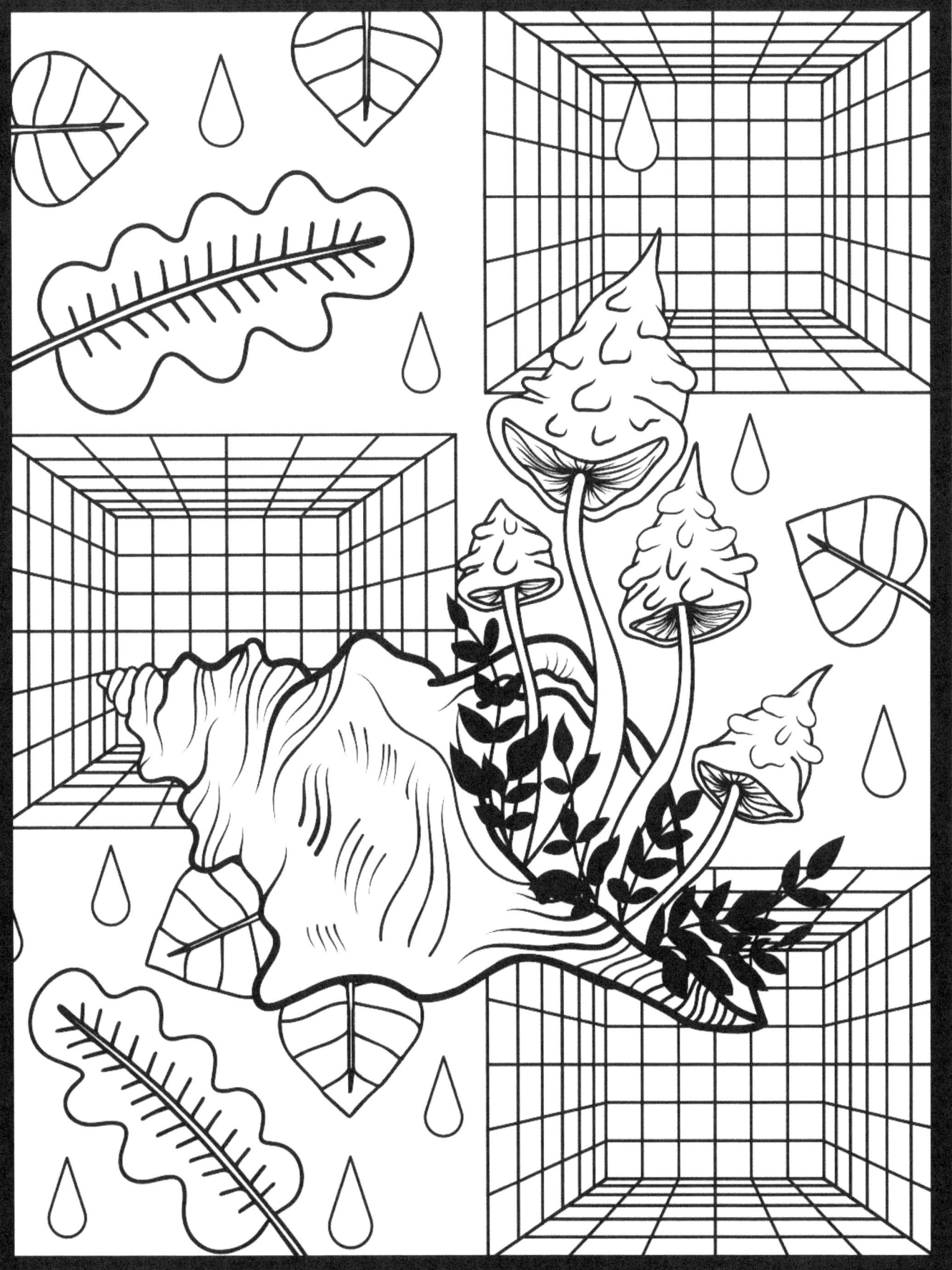

PHONE HOME

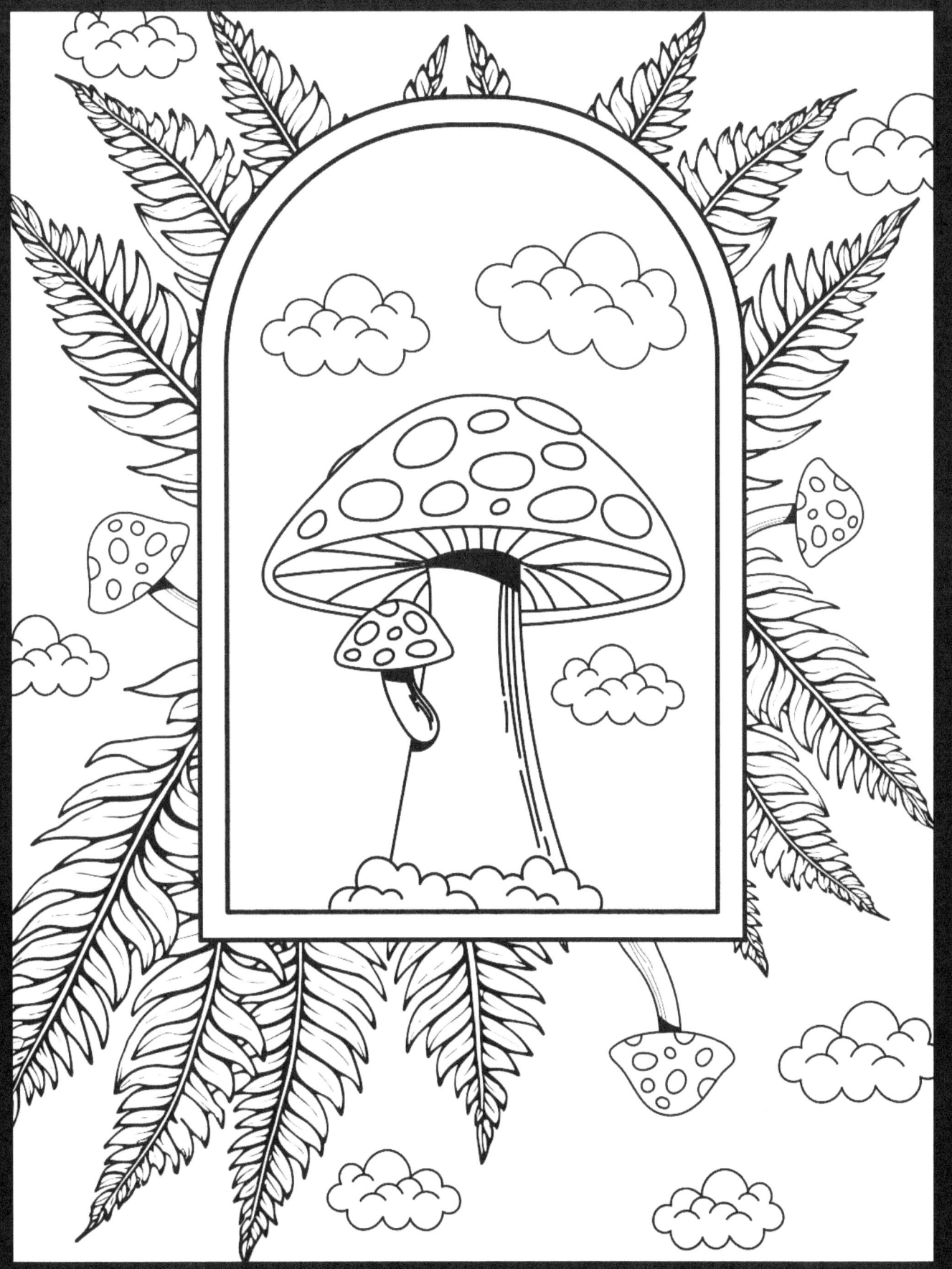

MUSHROOM PORTAL

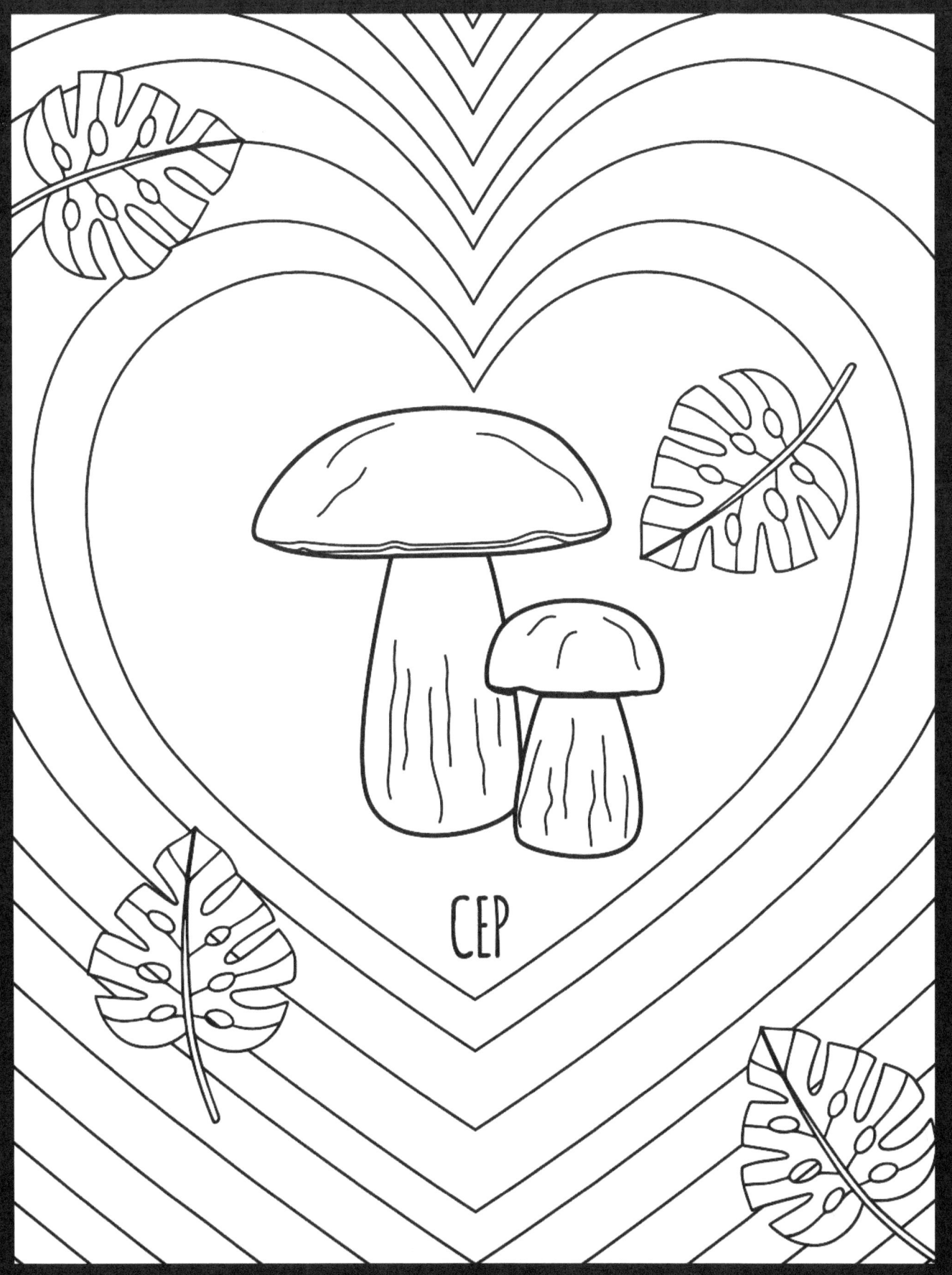

CEP

CEP

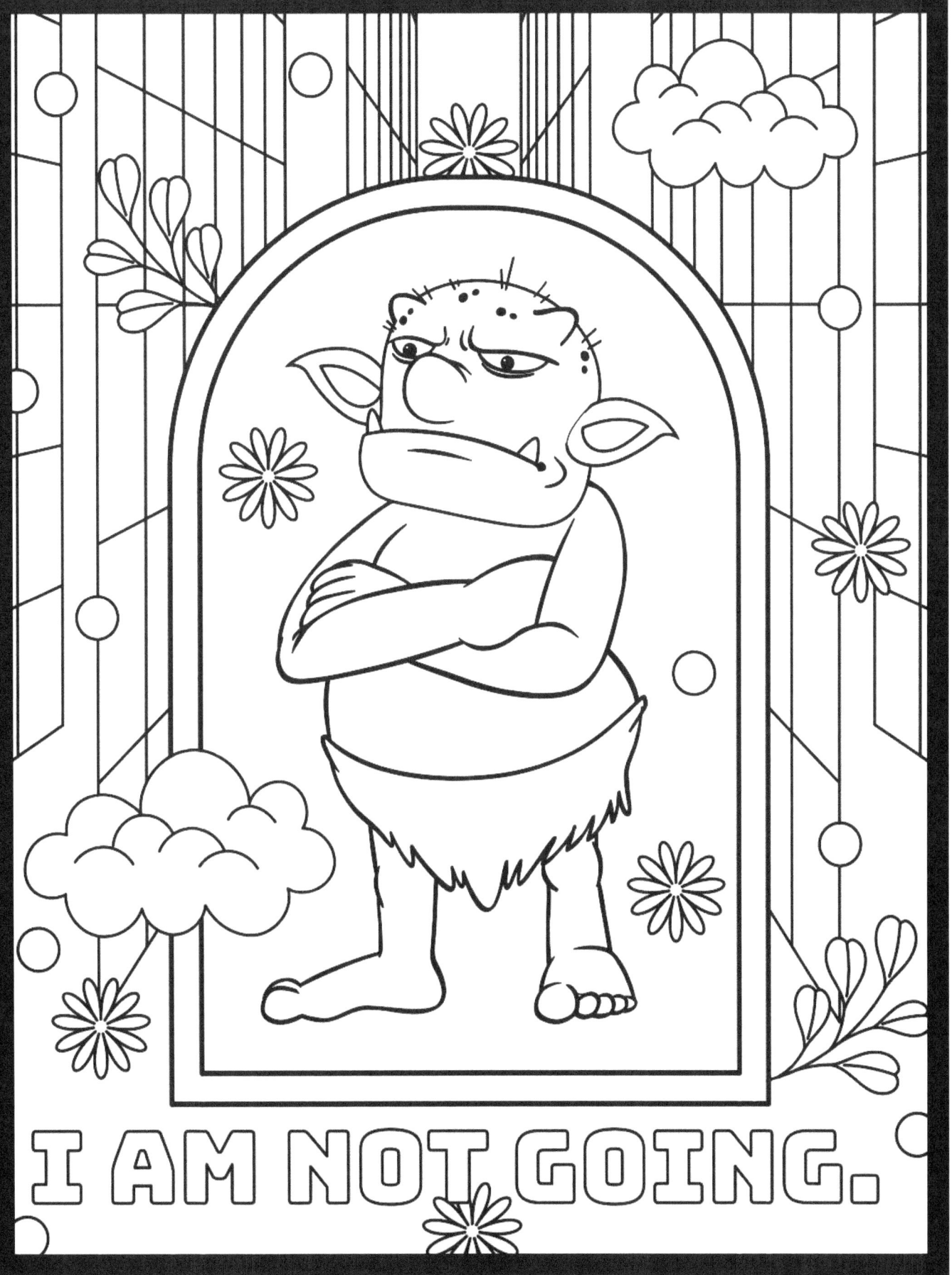

I AM NOT GOING

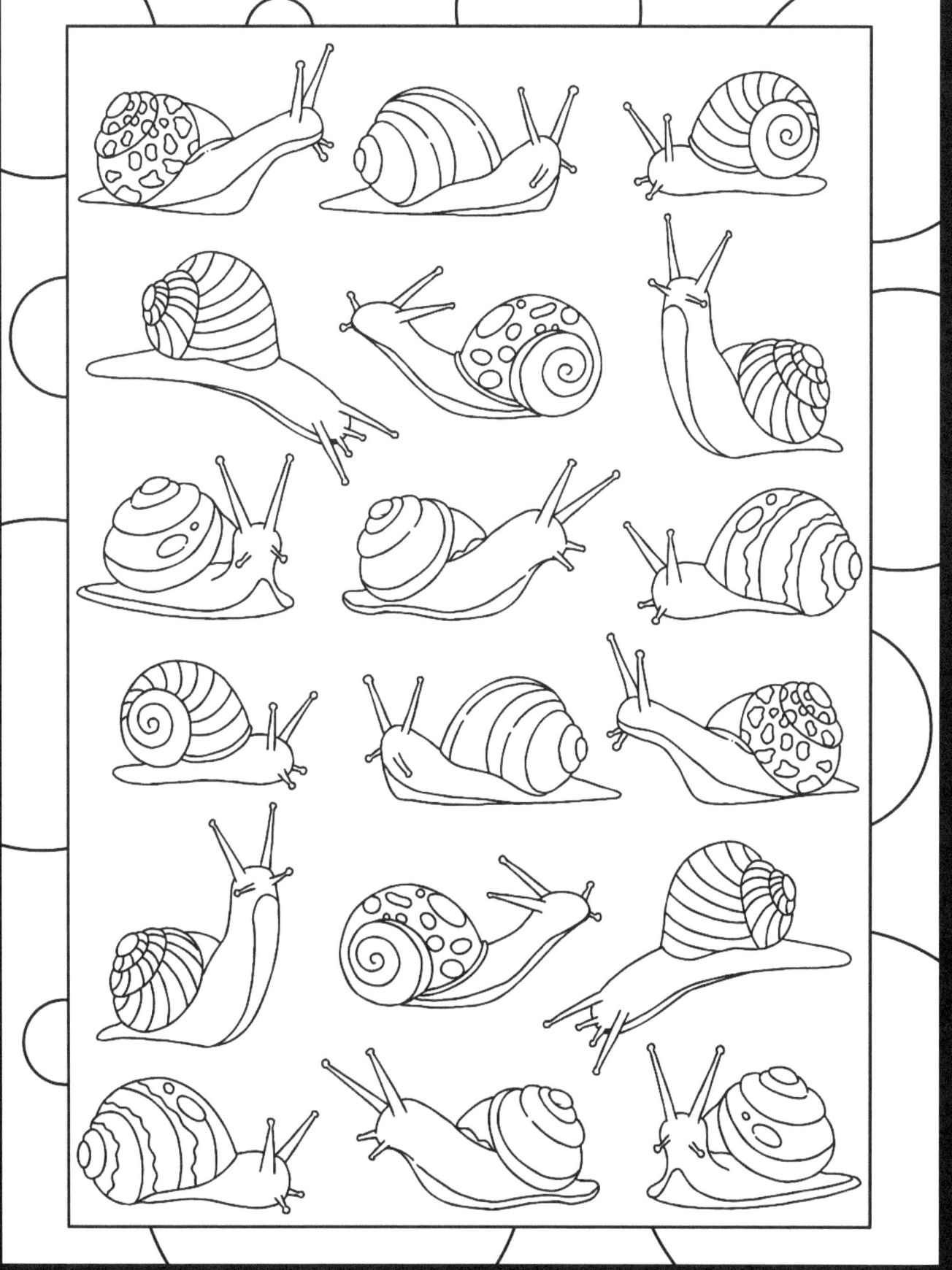

SNAILS

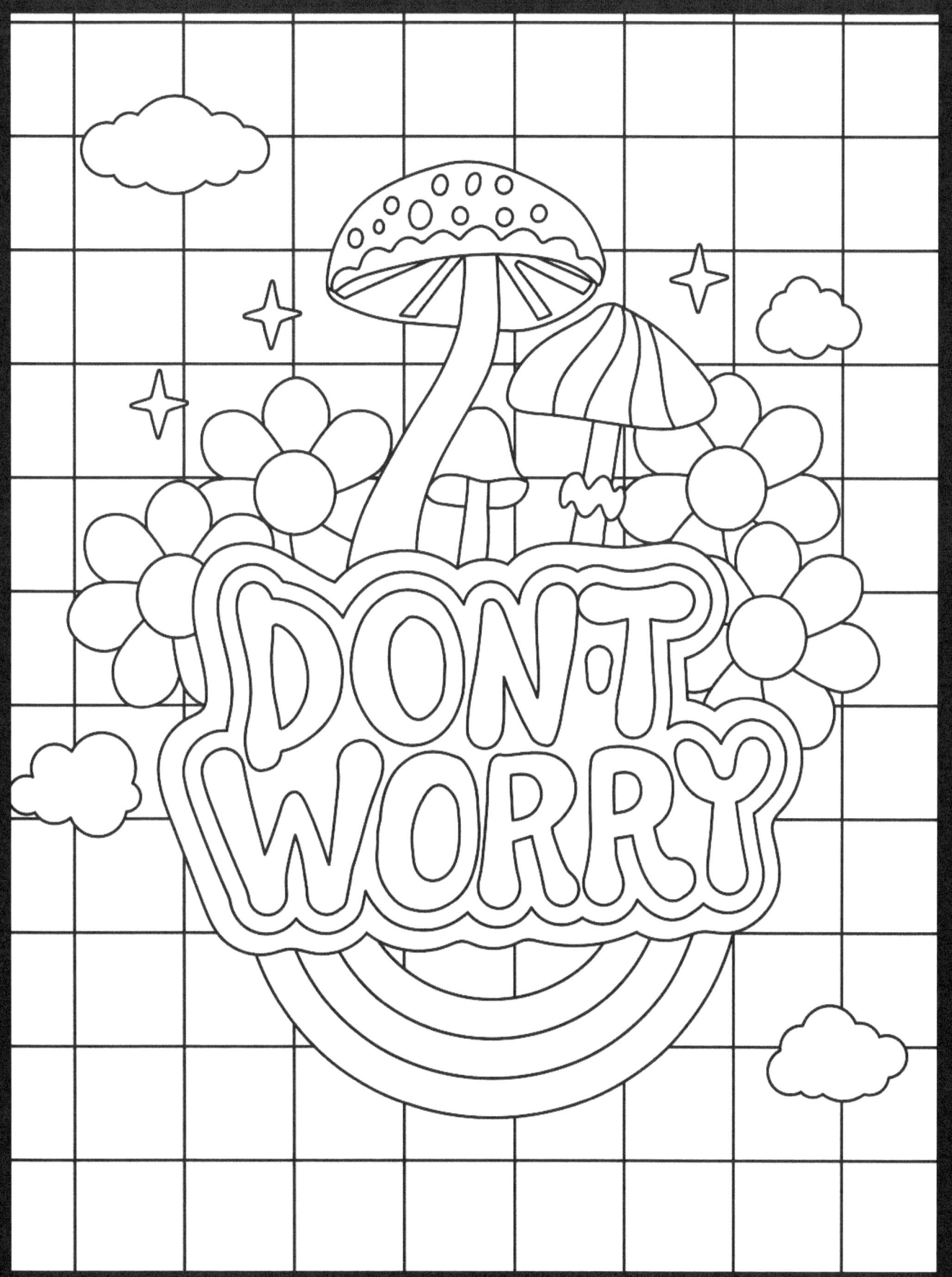

DON'T WORRY

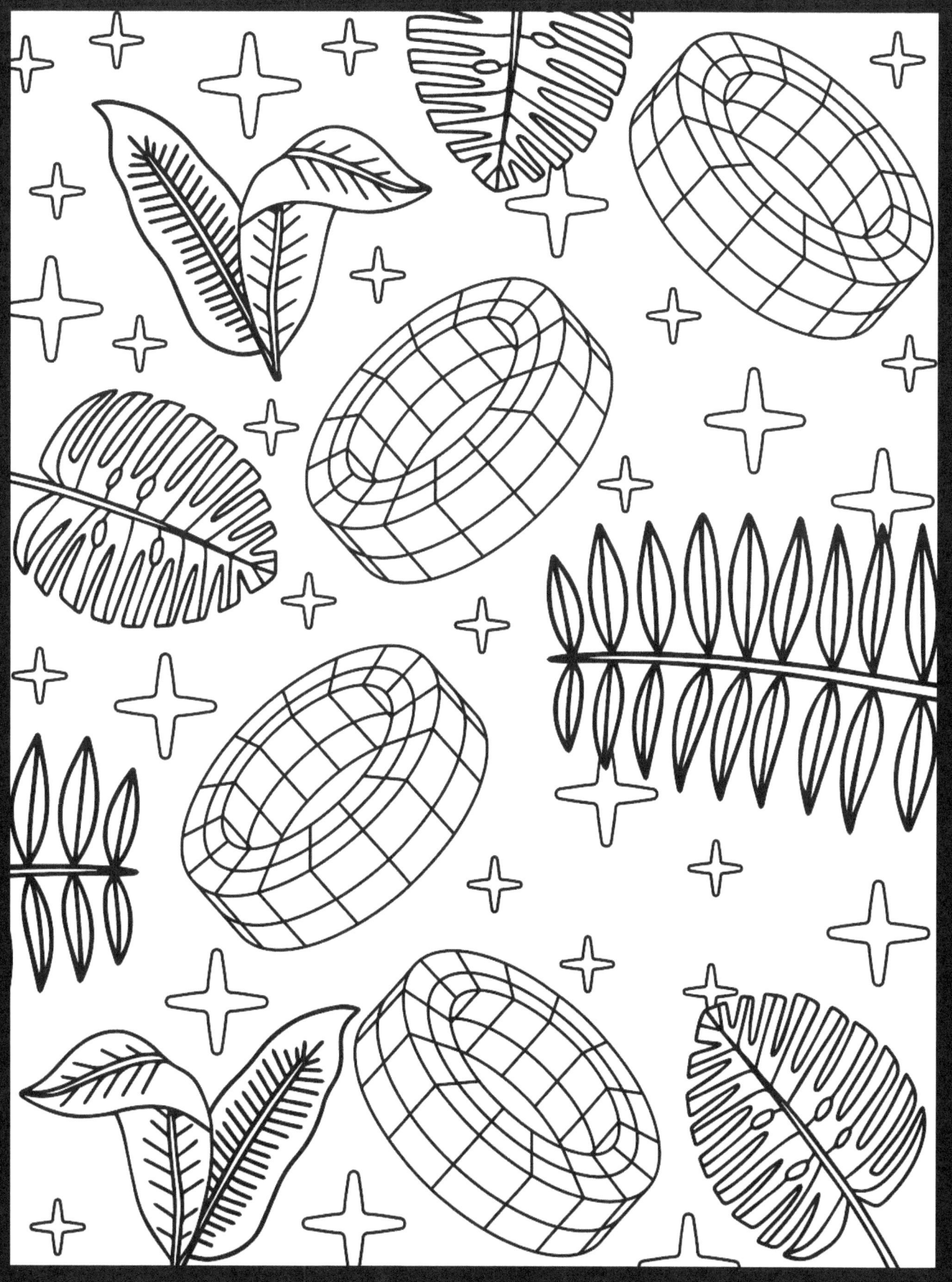

LOSS OF TIME

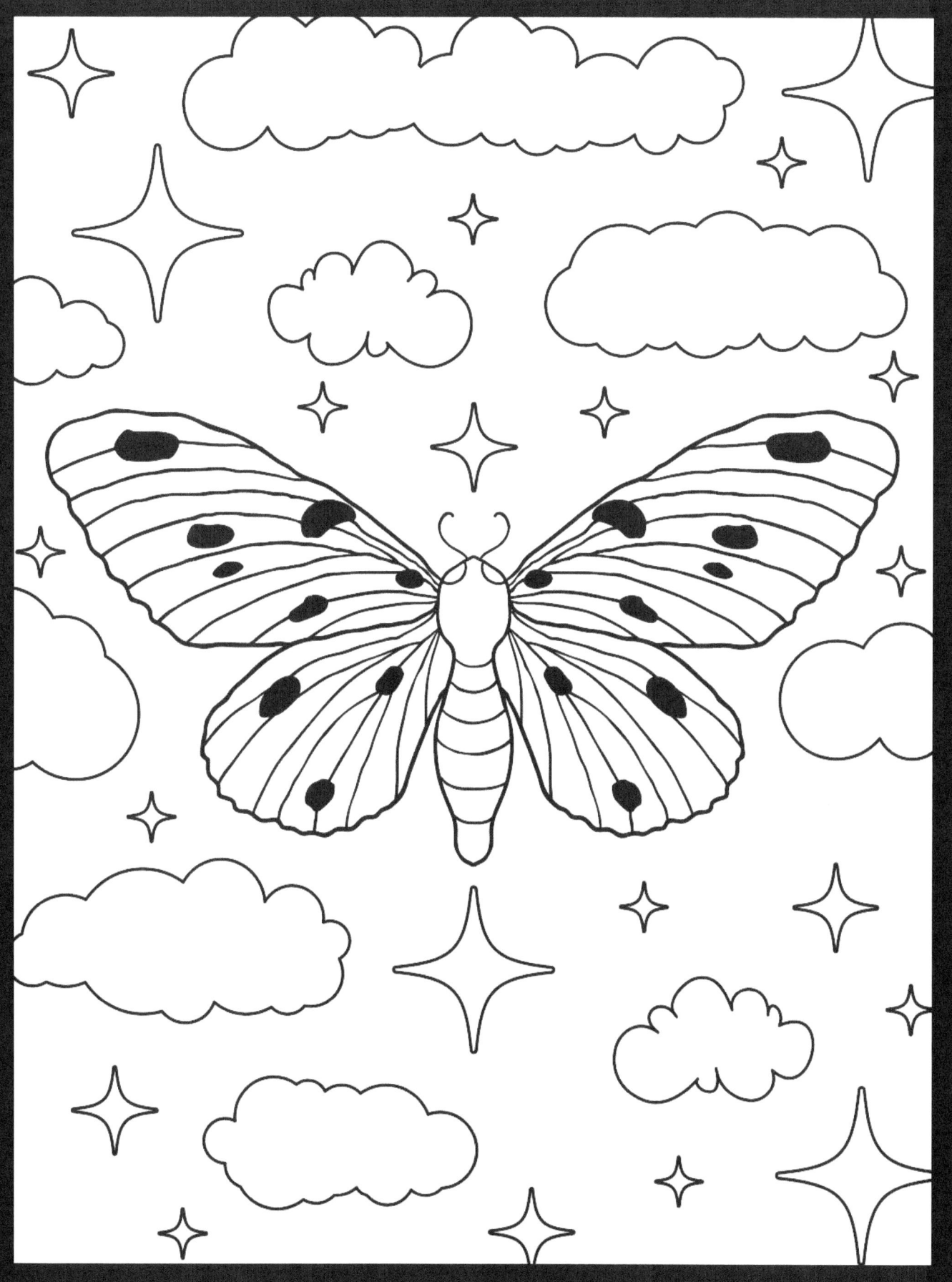

METAMORPHOSIS

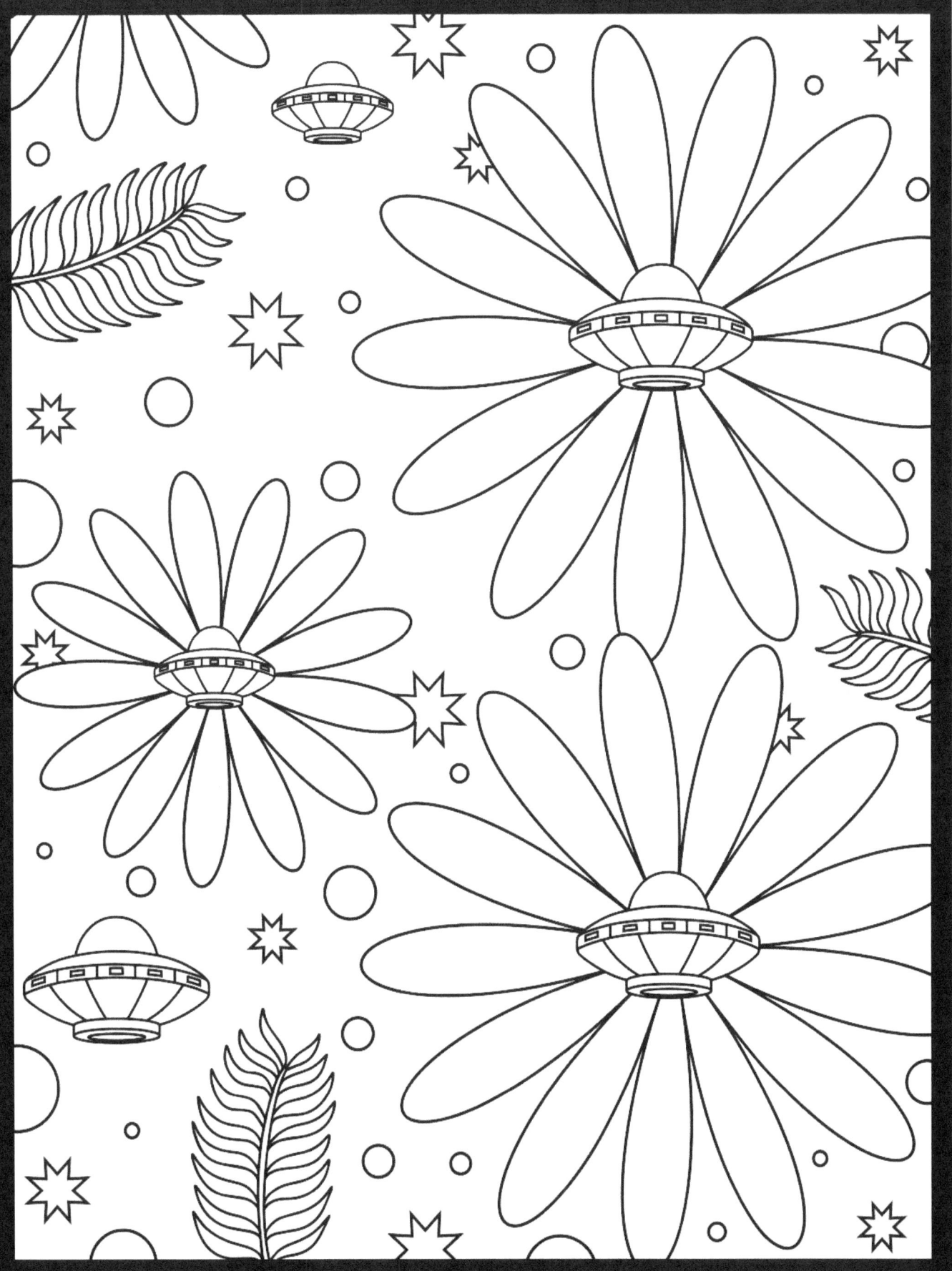

FLOWER POWER

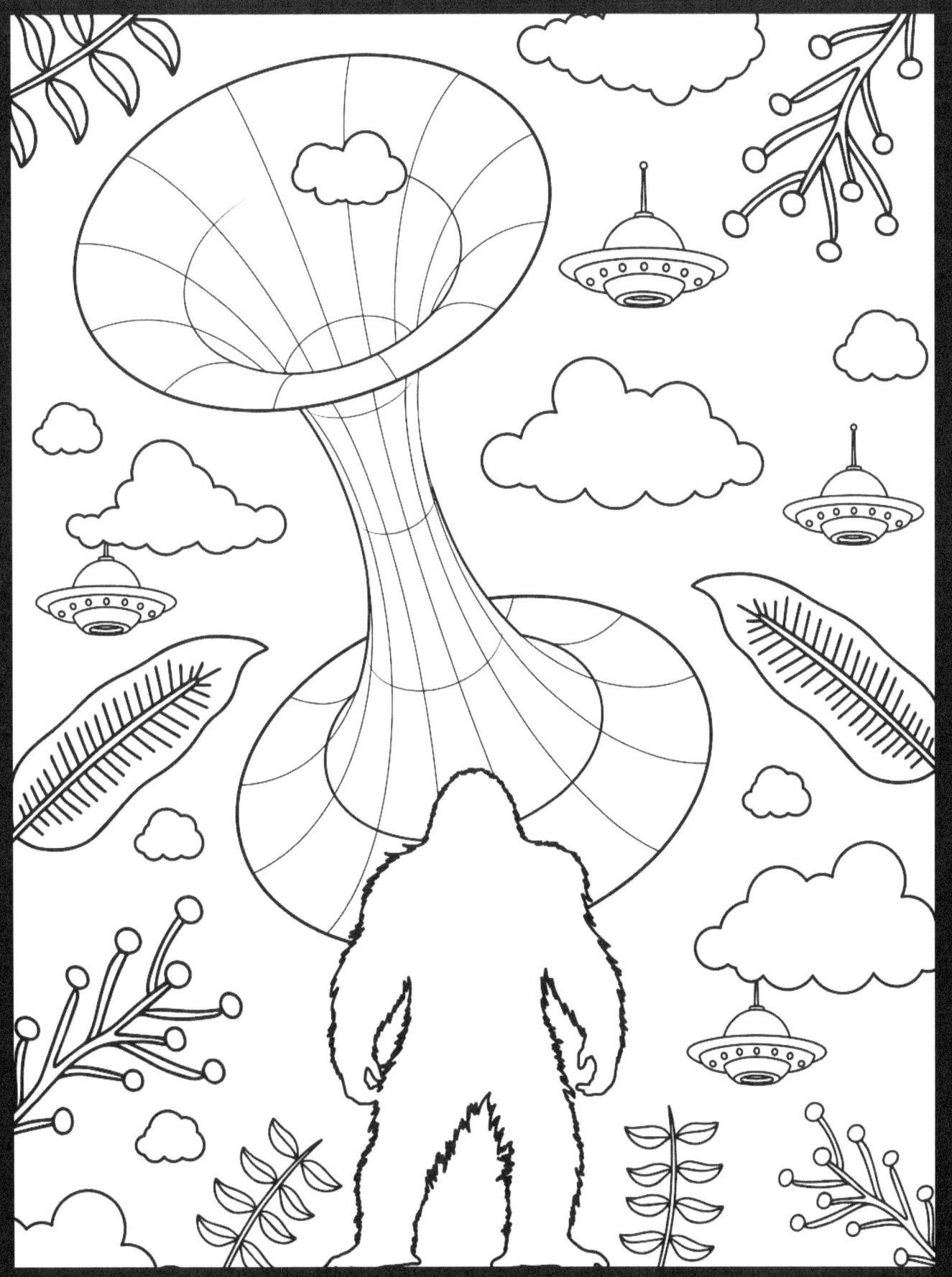

CONTACT

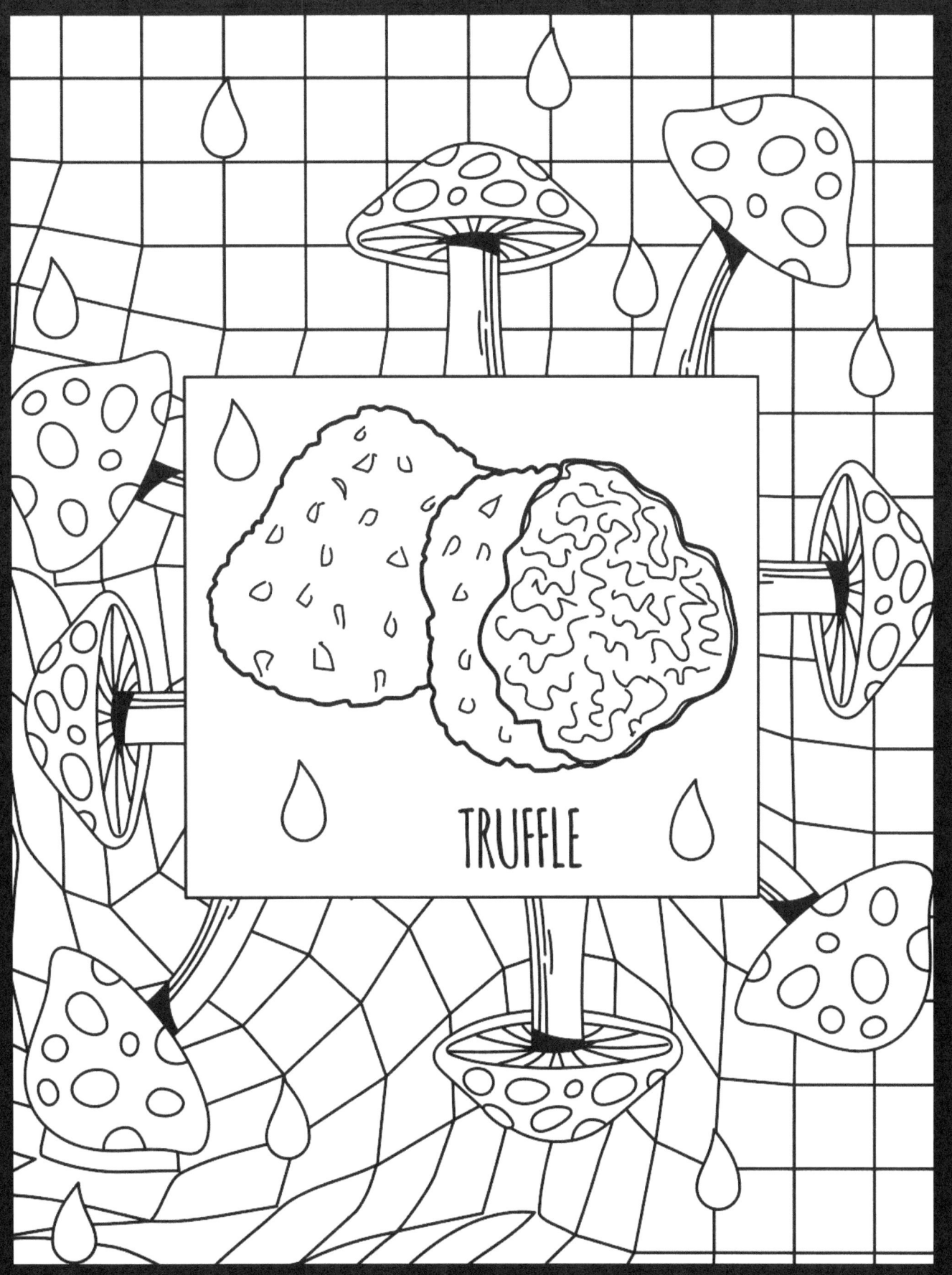

TRUFFLE

TRUFFLE

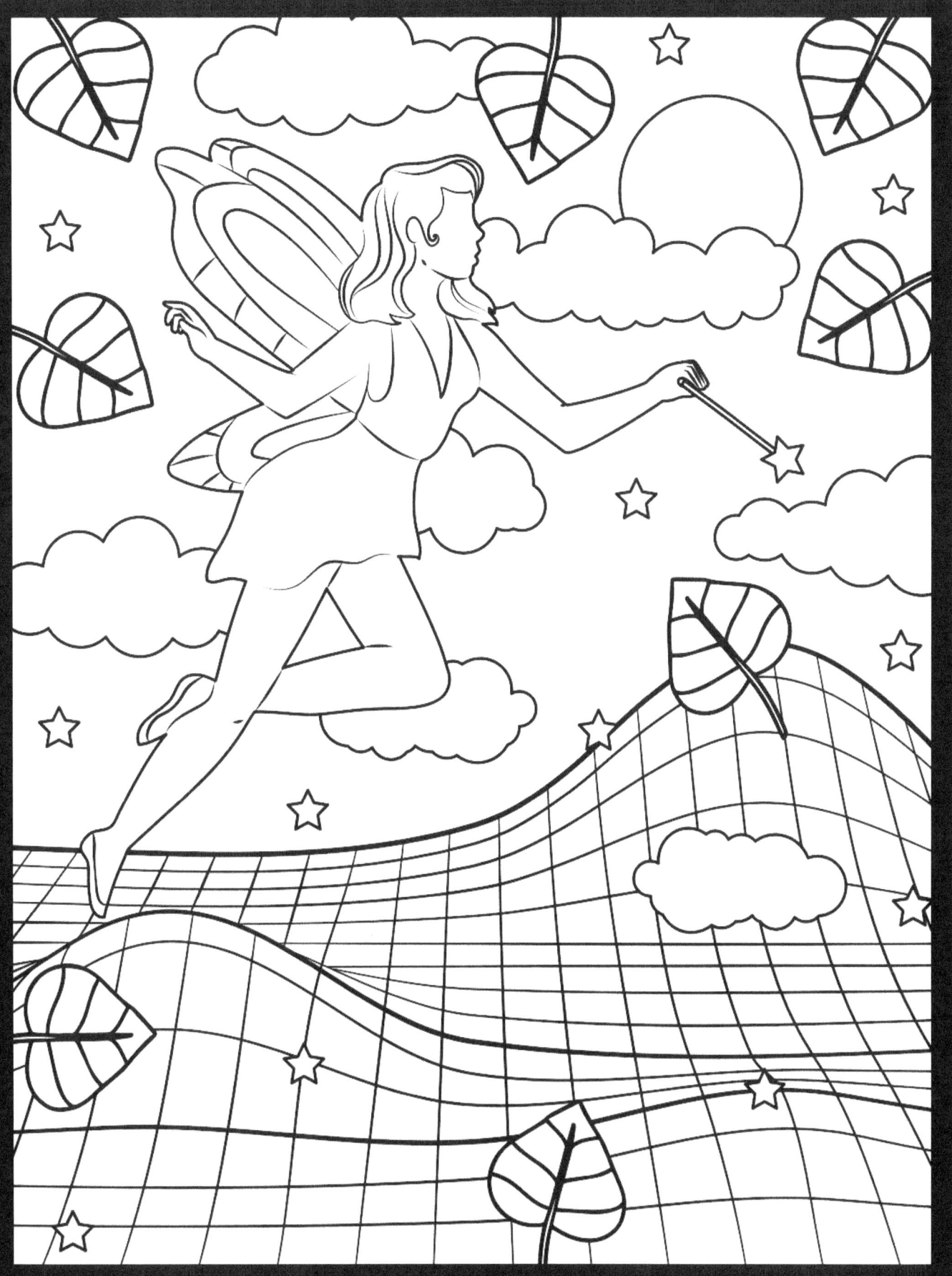

FAIRY

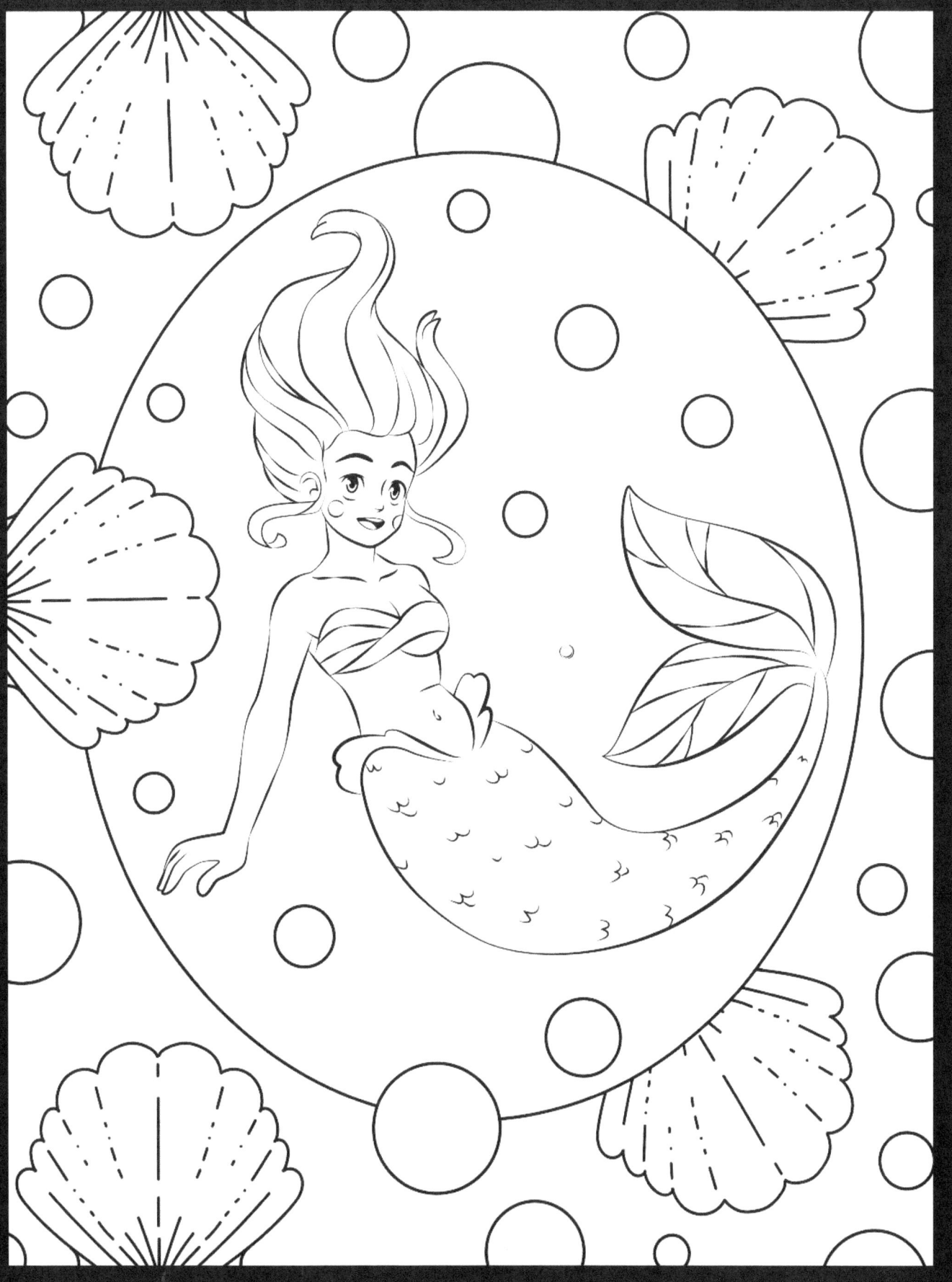

MERMAID

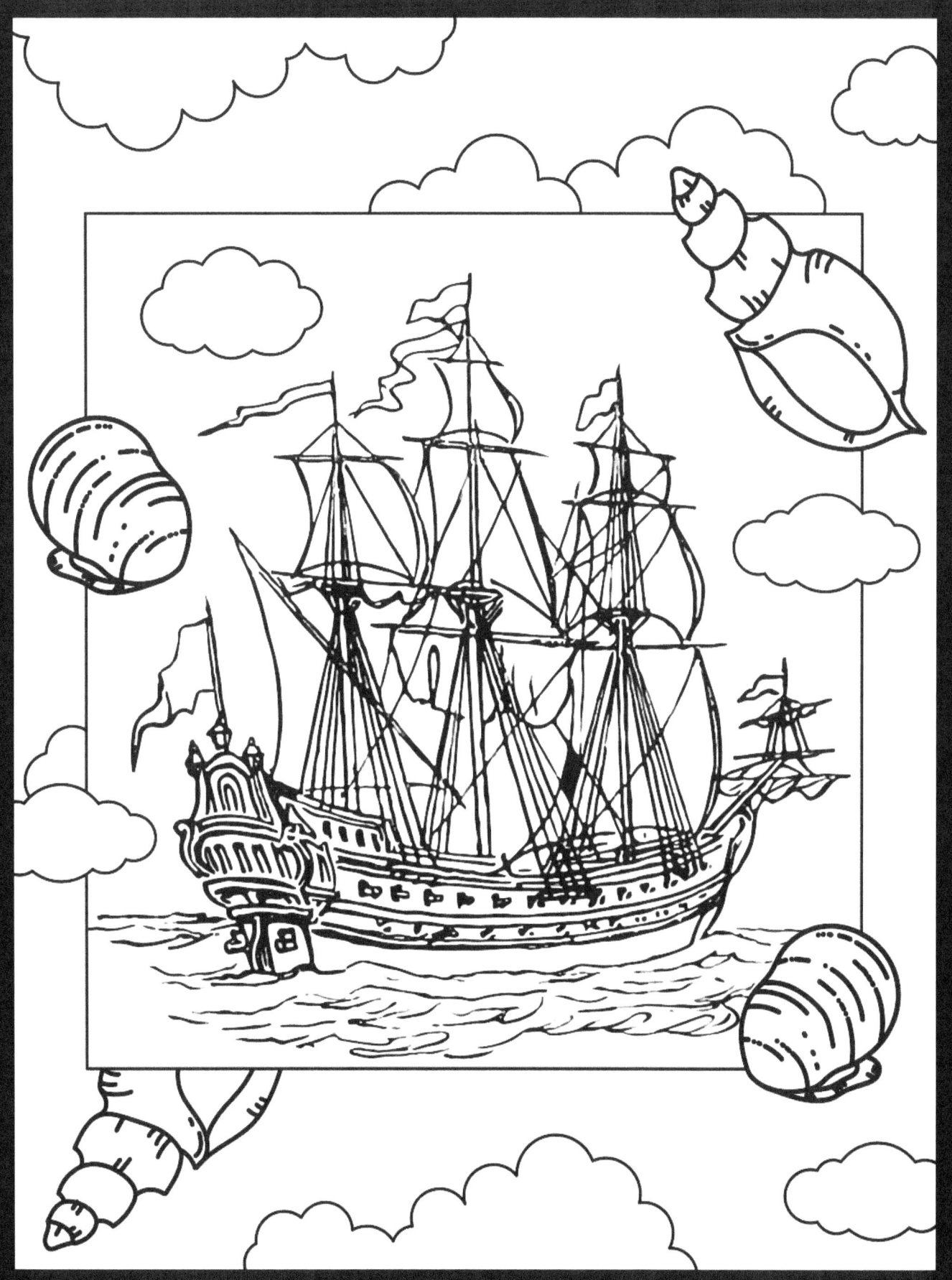

SAIL AWAY

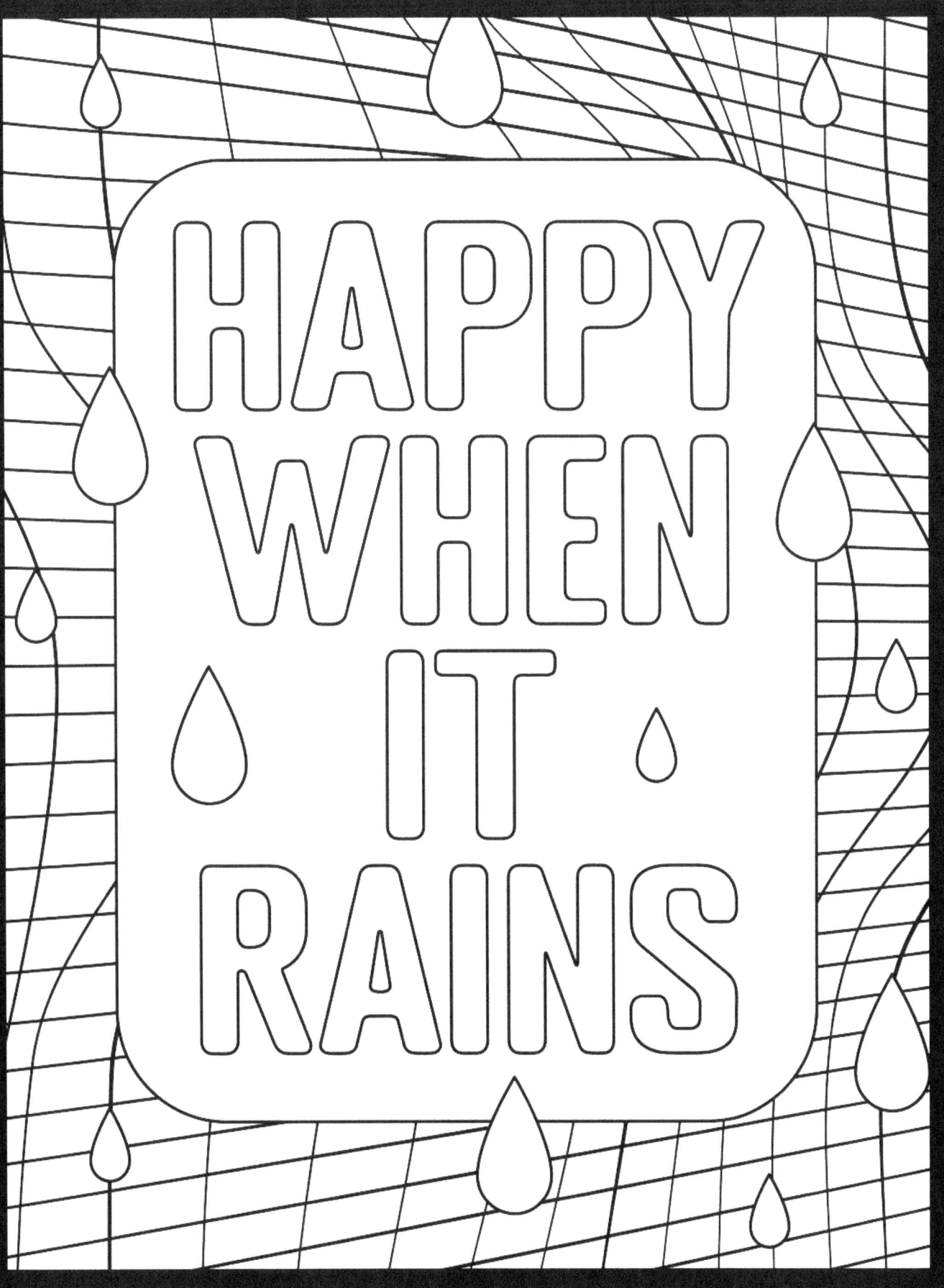

HAPPY WHEN IT RAINS

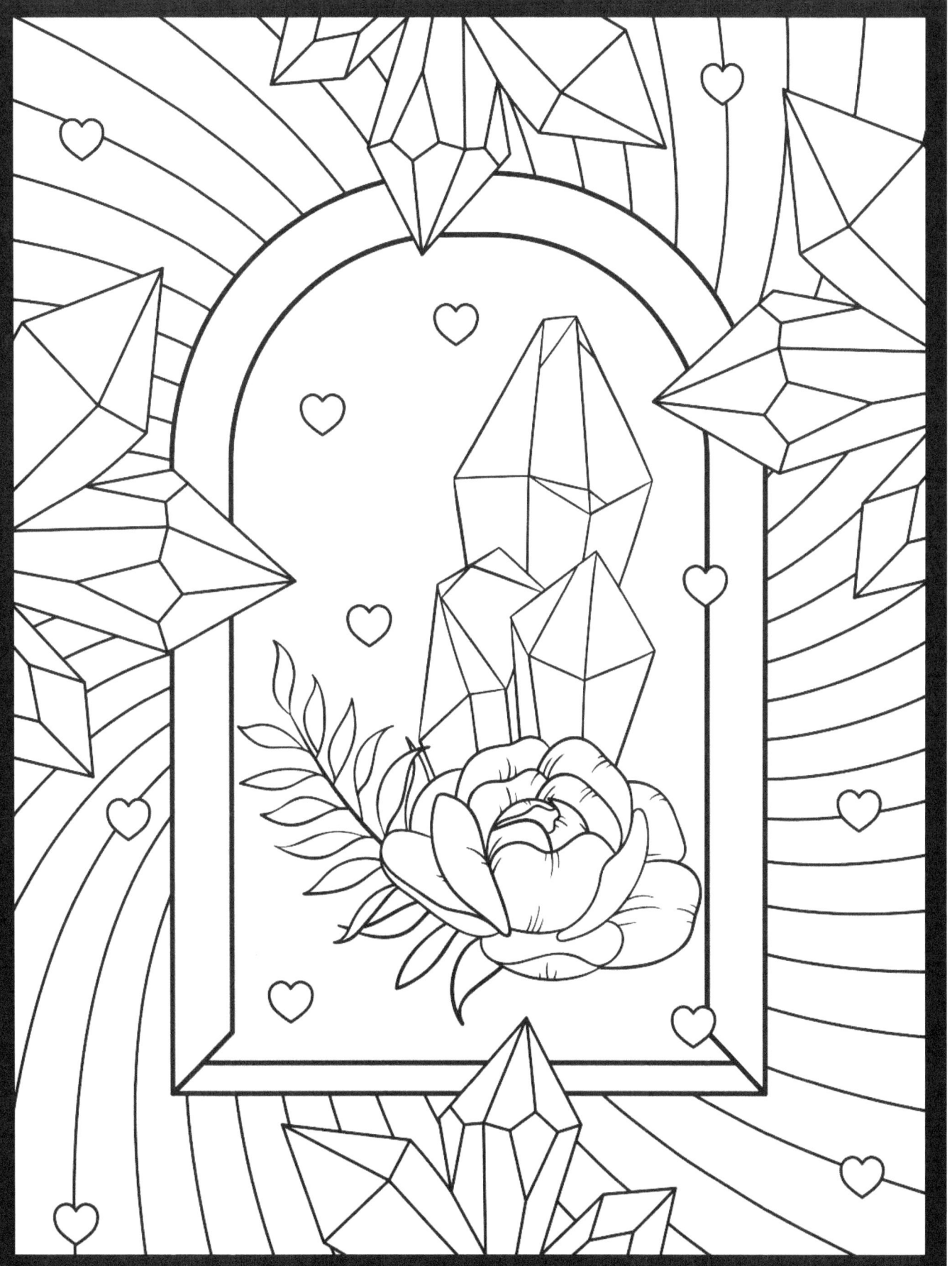

CRYSTAL KEYS

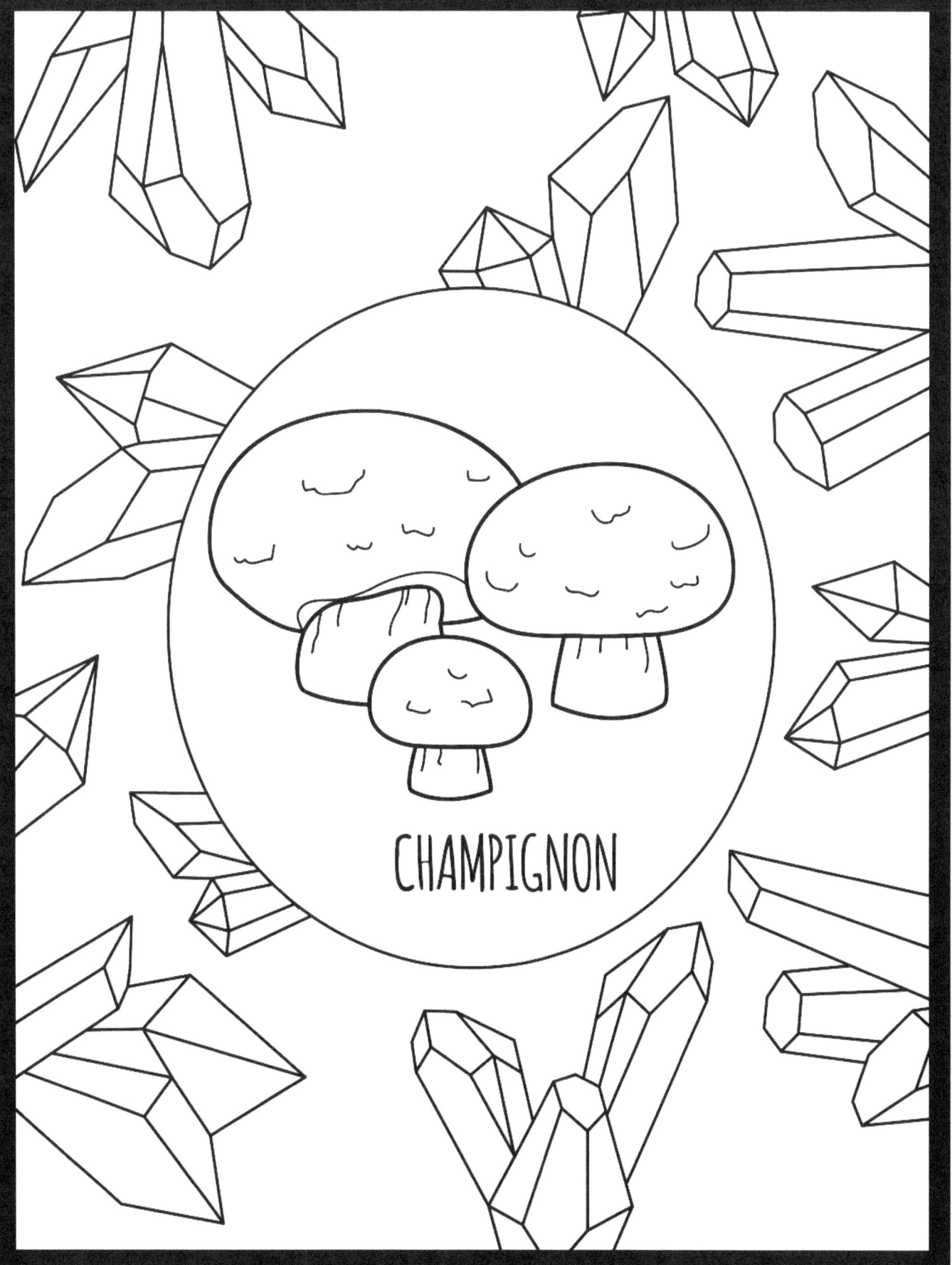

CHAMPIGNON

CHAMPIGNON

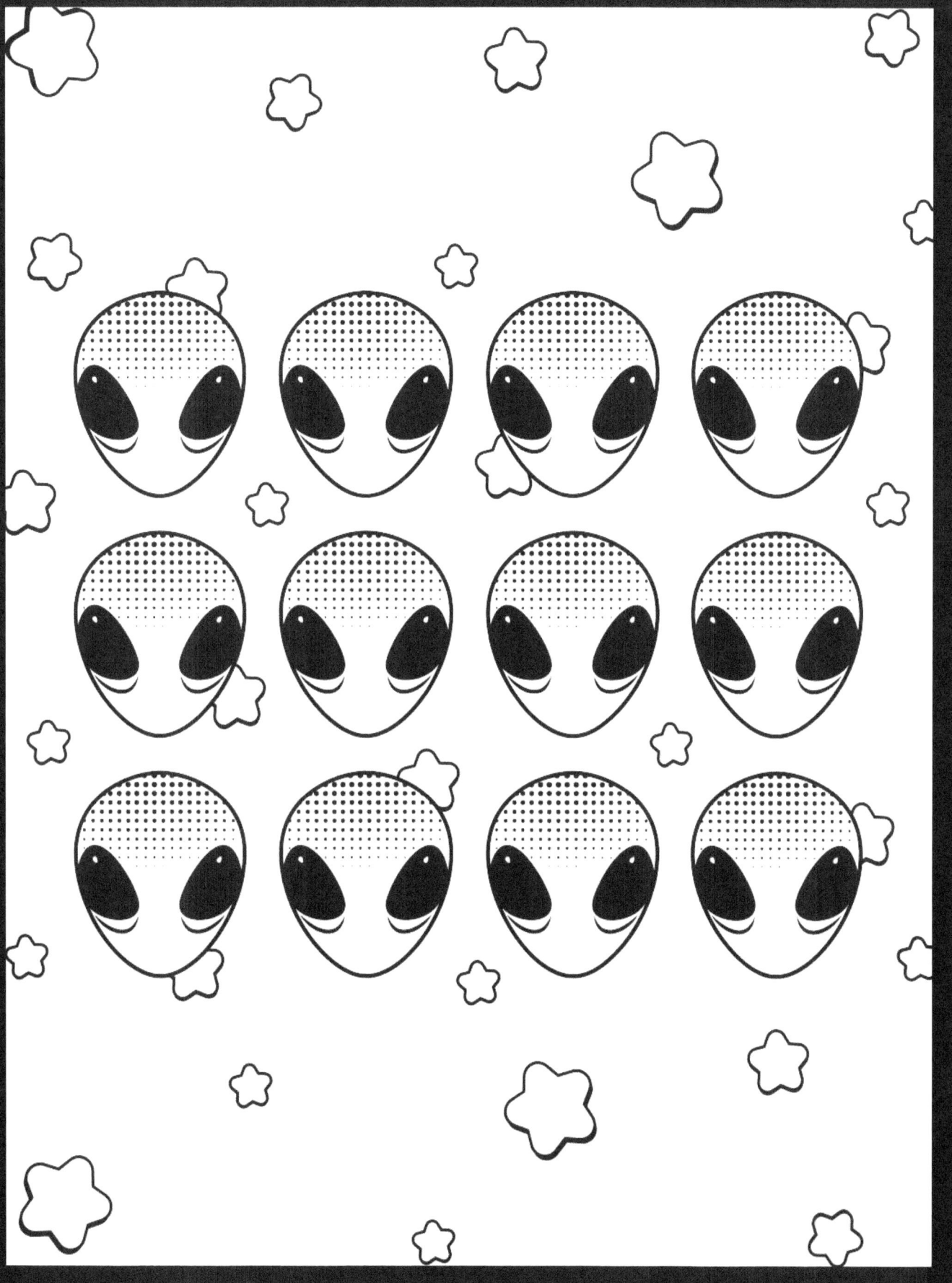

CUTIES

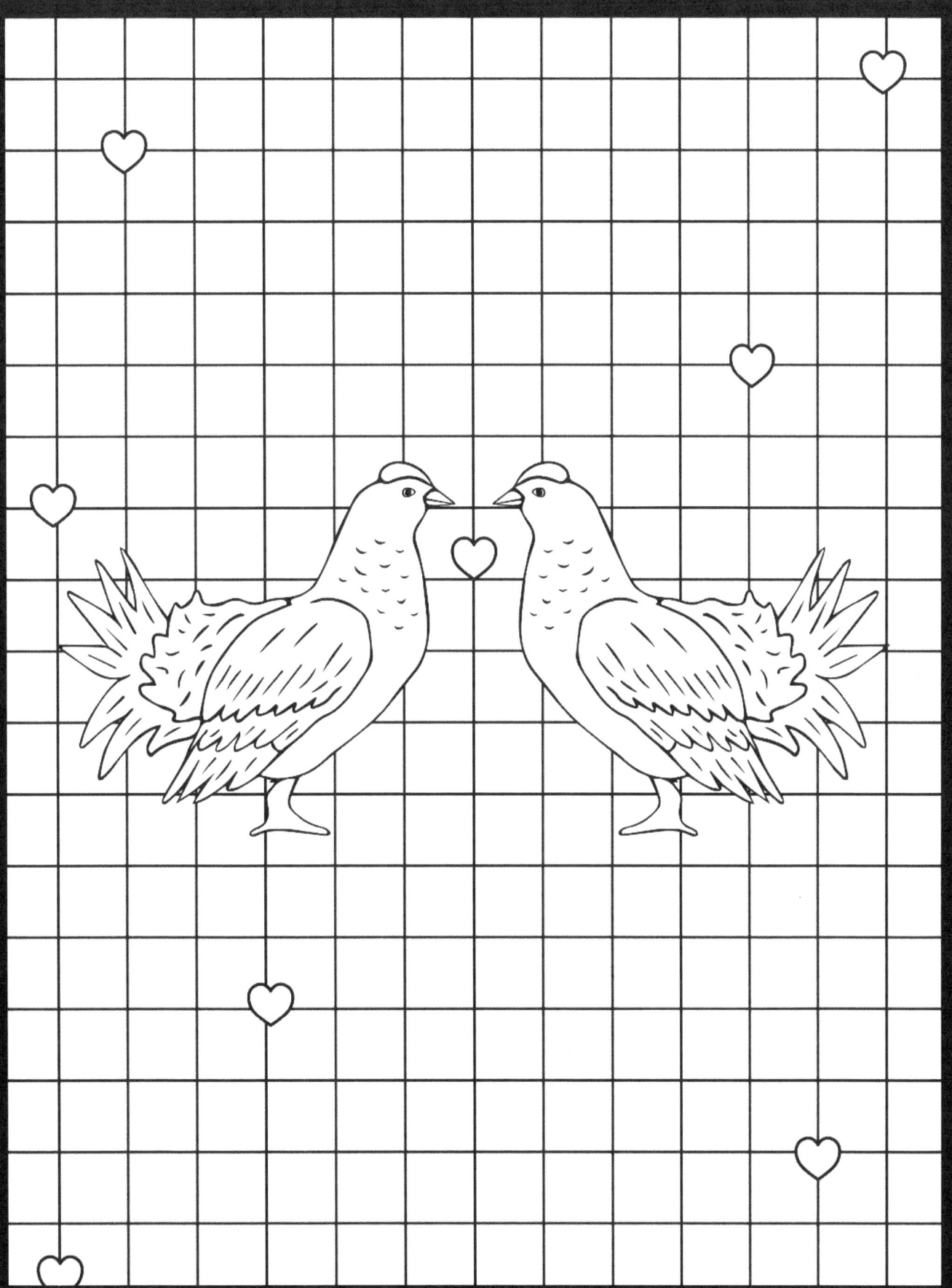

GROUSE

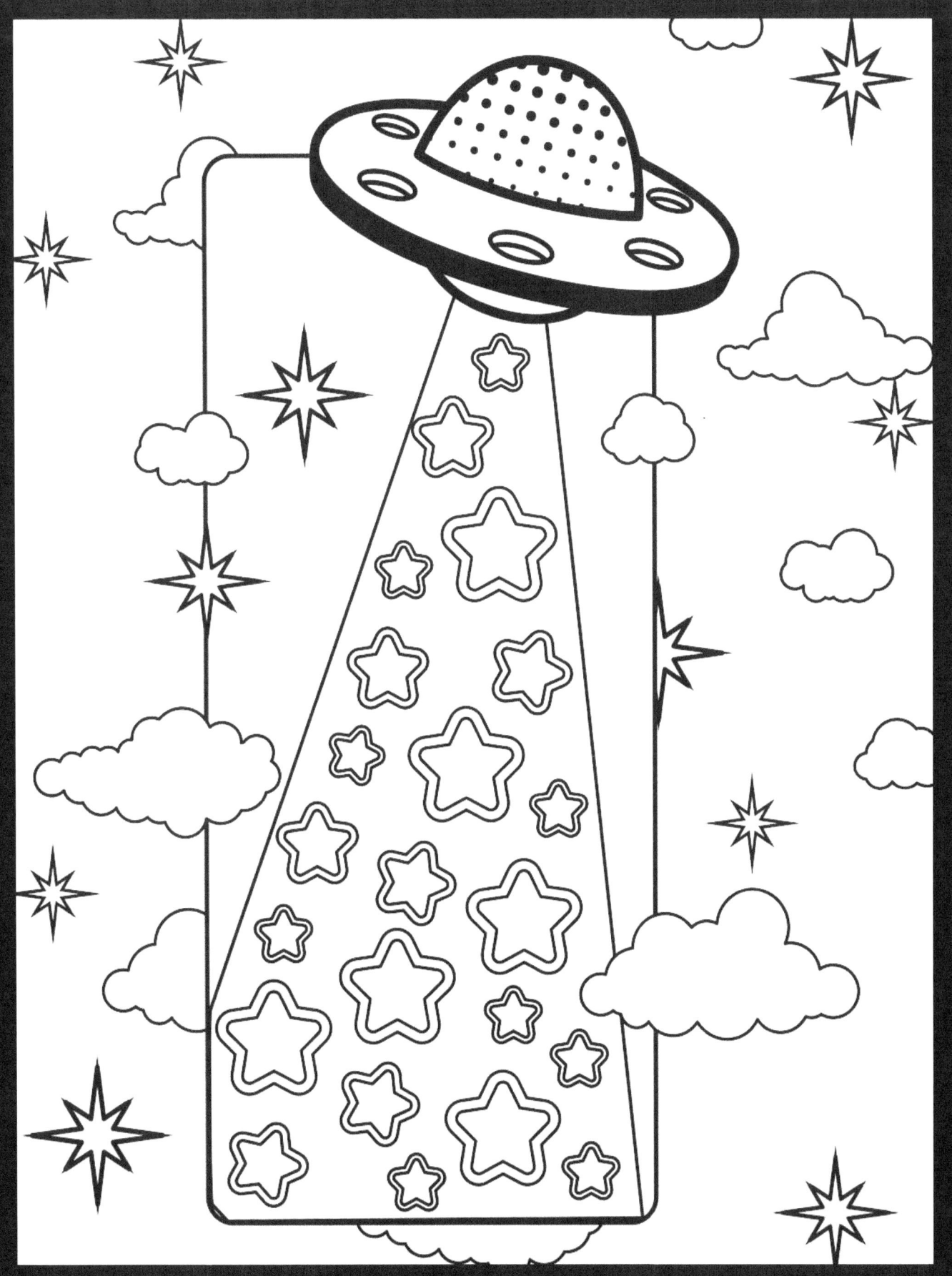

STARS

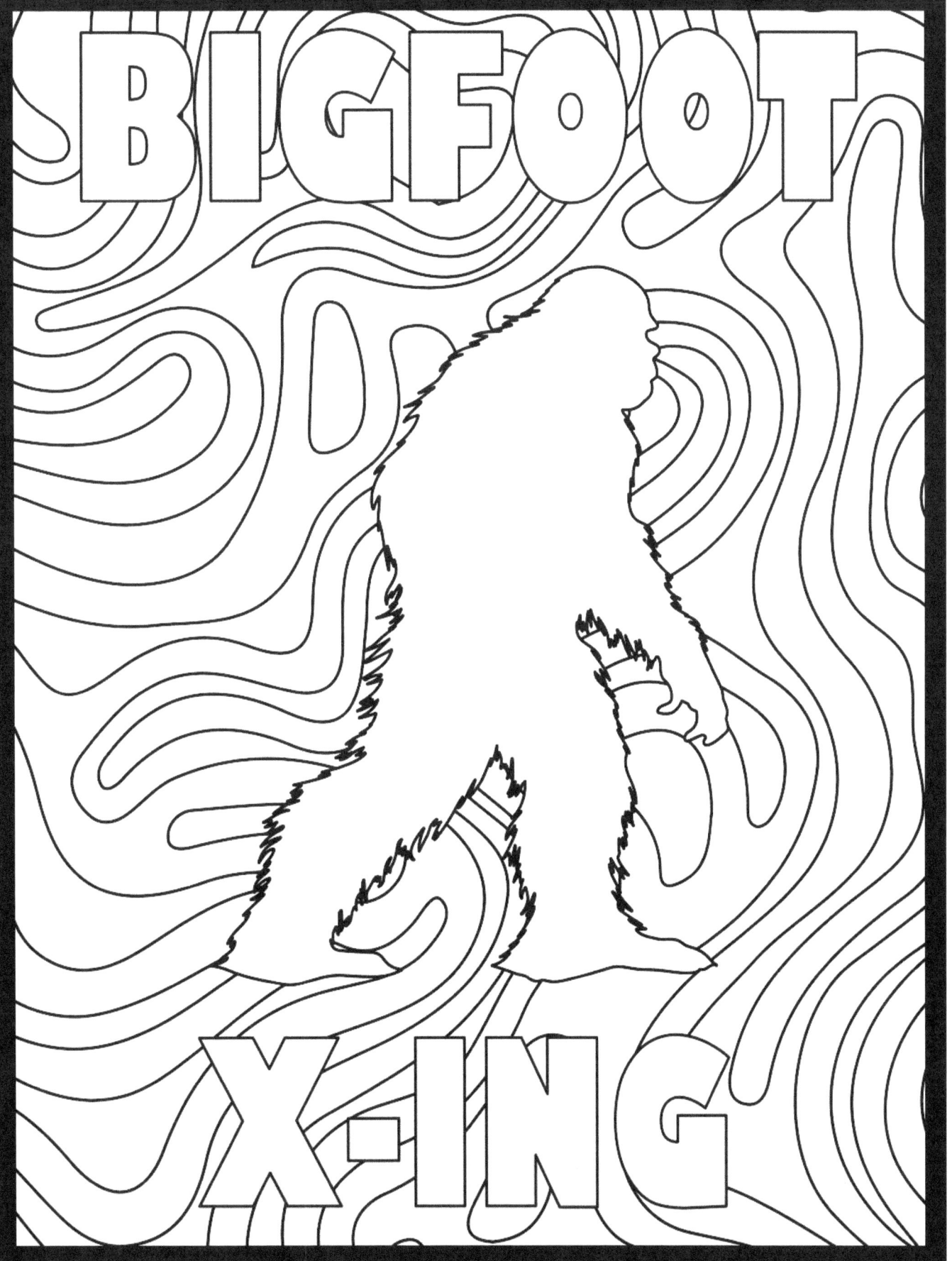

BIGFOOT CROSSING

COLLECT THEM ALL!

MORE BOOKS FROM

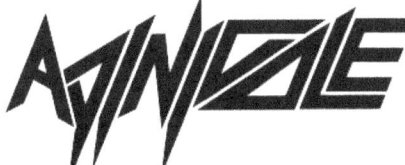

90S WAVE
DESERT DREAMS
HAUNTED HALLOWEEN
FRESH TO DEATH
METAMORPHOSIS
SPOOKSHOW
TRANSCENDENTAL TAROT
SUPERNATURAL SPLENDORS
SPACE JUNK
AWAKENING
LOVE SPELL
ETHEREAL GARDEN
AS ABOVE SO BELOW
FEELING FABULOUS
BEACH PLEASE
HOLIDAY HAPPENINGS
THE DIVINE FEMINIST
MYSTIC FOREST

THANK YOU!!